The Oldie
Annual 2024
Introduction
By Harry Mount, Editor, The Oldie

In his prescient poem, printed overleaf, in the first issue of *The Oldie*, A N Wilson hails the genius of our founding father, Richard Ingrams:

'When you and Private Eye were in your youth,
The oldies howled, because you told the truth.'

That has remained the case at *The Oldie*, ever since that first issue in 1992, under Richard and his much-missed successor as editor, Alexander Chancellor.

The Oldie tells the truth – not in some po-faced, humourless, pontificating way. But through witty, sad, brainy articles by the best writers over the past 30-plus years.

That's why editing *The Oldie* is the best job in Fleet Street. With one drawback – because some of our writers tend to have been around a while, they hit their final deadline all too often, pen still in hand. Just in the last two years, we've lost two of our greatest comic writers, who both happened to be called Barry.

Barry Cryer (1935-2022) was the finest of friends to *The Oldie*, as a contributor and as the MC at our literary lunches. You'll find one of his bottomless supply of jokes on the next page. Elsewhere in the annual, he salutes his fellow Old Fart in the Night, the late Willie Rushton.

When Barry Humphries (1934-2023) became a columnist for *The Oldie*, we got four writers for the price of one: Sir Les Patterson, Dame Edna Everage, Barry McKenzie and Barry himself. Fragrant Dame Edna graces this annual.

Barry Humphries often asked me whether his columns outraged the readers. But one of the joys of *Oldie* readers is how unshockable they are. The only letter I got criticising Sir Les Patterson said, 'I cannot believe you employ this disgusting Australian – and it's staggering that he's been appointed Cultural Attaché to the Court of St James.' Barry loved the idea that someone thought Sir Les was for real. Roger Lewis says farewell to dear Barry in these pages.

Again and again in this annual – edited with sublime taste and wit by Jane Mays – you'll find writers who operate on the two Barrys' higher plane, built on irony, satire, mock rudeness and all the verbal elements that lift sentences above the everyday.

Here you'll find Auberon Waugh on death – and why Lord Dawson, George V's doctor, should have been hanged for treason after delivering too much morphine into his jugular artery.

Here is Germaine Greer, another Wizard from Oz, on her beloved Cambridgeshire beeches being struck down by the wild west wind.

Many of the peerless contributors here and many featured interviewees – Sir John Mortimer, Edward Enfield and Kathleen Hale, creator of Orlando the Marmalade Cat – are no more.

But many of the writers are still going strong in the magazine today: John McEwen, *The Oldie*'s Bird of the Month columnist, and the column's illustrator Carry Akroyd; Elisabeth Luard; and Giles Wood, our Country Mouse, now a *Gogglebox* star with his wife, Mary Killen, our beauty columnist.

And what jewels our correspondents bring back from their travels – and their youth. How astonishing to hear that the quintessential youngie-oldie, Nicky Haslam, handed Marilyn Monroe the contacts of a heart-breakingly lovely photograph of her only weeks before her death in 1962: 'The mascara-messed eyes look up at me, her voice strangely remote...'

All human life is here. Well, all interesting, sad and funny human life is here.

'I think they want us to leave'

Published by The Oldie magazine, Moray House, 23/31 Great Titchfield Street, London W1W 7PA www.theoldie.co.uk
Copyright © 2023 Oldie Publications Ltd. Printed by Wyndeham Roche Ltd
The Oldie would like to thank all the writers, illustrators and cartoonists whose work is reproduced in these pages
Editor: Jane Mays **Design:** Jonathan Anstee and Christina Richmond **Cover:** Ed McLachlan

Contents

102

74

93

In the beginning...

Oldie Founding Father: Richard Ingrams

A poetic welcome to *The Oldie* by A N Wilson

Ingrams Encore

Sir: When you and *Private Eye*
    were in your youth,
The oldies howled, because
    you told the truth
About the humbug world
    which *Baillie Vass*
Tried to protect with
    money or with class.
Young *Ingrams, Marnham,*
    Rushton, Foot and *Waugh*
Gleefully wove old
    England's winding sheet,
Unveiled *Profumo's* lies,
    Wilson's clay feet,
The sins of *Maxwell, Thorpe*
    and many more.
Some of your heroes then
    are now so old
That they are dead and
    cannot be enrolled
To write for you, but keep
    them in your mind
Lest, mellowing in age, you

should grow kind.
Don't wage a war on youth,
    which will outgrow
Its childish follies –
    rather, raise a cry
Against the shyster
    lawyers, the MPs,
The flannel-bishops, the
    performing fleas
Whom you lambasted
    yearly in *The Eye*.
Remember *Cockburn's*
    cruel vision, which
Made him distrust the
    Tories and the rich.
When tempted to admire
    some oldie shit
Puncture his vanity with
    Driberg's wit.
When sentiment would
    lure you to invest
Belief in humbugs, I would
    beg you lift

From *Malcolm Muggeridge*
    his greatest gift: the
    inability to be impressed.
Your enemies believe
    you're off your trolley:
Glory in that! And rage
    at this world's folly.
And laugh at Death and,
    with no trace of fear
Mock gilded butterflies,
    like old *King Lear*.
If, armed with writs, disgusted
    Middle Age
Hires *Carter-Ruck* to close
    The Oldie down,
Then, you've succeeded!
    Everyone in town
Will cheer an *Ingrams* encore
    on the stage.

A N Wilson
*This ode to Richard Ingrams
was in the first issue in 1992*

The last joke by
Barry Cryer (1935-2022)

A man is at his wife's funeral in the local crematorium
He asks the vicar, 'What's the Wi-Fi password here?'
The vicar says, 'It's your wife's funeral!'
And the man says, 'Is that all lower case?'

(Spooky, but this is just the page you were looking for)

Hello, Possums!

Readers are always bombarding me with questions, and when you're an international role model like me - an icon, for heaven's sake! - you are duty bound, within reason, to satisfy the public's insatiable curiosity. You'd be amazed, for instance, how many happily married men want to know my birthstone, my favourite novelist (Anita Brookner), my inside leg measurement, and my sexual fantasies.

Now, with Christmas just a memory, readers with nothing better to do are besieging me with letters asking if I got their pathetic cards and trumpery gifts and begging to know where I spent the festive season. I warn my readers that mail does take a while to reach me since it is all X-rayed and sanitised by loyal members of my staff at Ednacare, Switzerland, the nerve centre of my organisation, and it is then forwarded to me at my lovely pink Spanish-style mansion in Beverly Hills.

In Beverly Hills, incidentally, people don't say 'Merry Christmas', but 'Happy Holidays', and Christmas trees are called 'Holiday Trees' in this rather spooky part of the world. Even though I am probably Jewish, I tend to draw the line at that.

The Chrissie symbol here seems to be my least favourite shrub, the poinsettia, and I don't remember any mention of that ghastly weed in my New Testament. But quite frankly, I always adored Christmas in most of my incarnations, except the one yucky Yuletide when I was burned at the stake - but that's another story.

Actually, on Christmas day, I was in Aspen, Colorado, and I naturally went to church. It was one of those American religious events specially designed so as not to embarrass heathens. There were several carols tastefully edited so as not to offend atheists, devil-worshippers, lepers, tinted folk and disabled gays, but they were set to tunes I had not heard before in this life or any other! It wasn't exactly Muzak but what I would call 'Jeezak'. There was a funny atmosphere in the church and it was the sort of place where, if I had been a man (God forbid!), I wouldn't have felt like taking off my hat.

Not that the menfolk wear hats any

I adored Christmas in most of my incarnations - except the one yucky Yuletide when I was burned at the stake

more these days, do they? I well remember my wonderful late father never went out without a nice Akubra fedora snugly encasing his brilliantined brown. He always took it off in lifts too, I recall, which is something you absolutely never see these days unless it's William Powell or Cary Grant in black and white late at night. I think if more young people watched black-and-white films, they'd learn a lot more nice old-world manners, with the possible exception of Battleship Potemkin and the Cabinet of Dr Caligari. Akubra hats, incidentally, were stylish Australian scalp apparel made from compressed rabbit fur, and the word 'Akubra' is Latin for compressed rabbit, or indeed, jugged hare. There are Tibetan monks whose headgear is made from the shaved or plucked body hairs of their female saints. Just as well my hirsute bridesmaid Madge Allsop is not attached to a Tibetan monastery or they would soon be able to open a wholesale millinery business.

Before my skiing holiday recedes too far into the past, I should tell my readers that I am no James Bond floozie when it comes to the slopes, but I rather like the

social life of little nooks like Aspen, and I bumped into lots of old apres-ski pals like Dudley Moore, Chevy Chase, Donald Trump, James Coburn, and Michelle Pfeiffer. Spookily enough, I even collided with a gorgeous little producer from the Golden Days of the West End who put on my very first successful London show. His name was, and is, Michael White and when I stumbled upon him in the bimbo-upholstered lobby of the Ritz Carlton, he was busy performing an exercise far more strenuous than skiing. The Pursuit of Youth. The wee darling made me feel quite exhausted.

'Networking' is just as important as skiing in this quaint snow-clad hideaway and people were scratching each other's eyes out to get into my entourage and be part of my inner circle. Frankly, Possums, I never realized I was so hot! I hear some of the stars are boycotting Aspen this season because of some law affecting opera designers, window-dressers, airline-ticket writers and deleted show-album collectors. I would have asked my son Kenny and his flatmate, Clifford Smail for more details of this evil and discriminatory legislation, but they were too busy launching their new Aspen skiwear outlet, Slalom and Gomorrah.

Incidentally, Hillary Clinton has taken to beeping my pager more often than the beleaguered and embattled Queen of England! I am trying to get her to stop wearing those plastic headbands which I thought had gone out with June Allyson and sockettes. And I must say she's a lot more amenable to my suggestions than dear Old Barbie Bush whom I could never completely ease out of polyester. At least Hillary has a waistline.

Her favourite expression, like everyone else's in the USA, is 'no problem'. They particularly say 'no problem' when you ask them to perform a task which is not only impossible,but beyond their comprehension. It may well become the Clinton mantra in the months to come. Since 'no problem' now denotes the insoluble, there is now no phrase in America to describe a situation in which no problem whatsoever exists.

Incidentally I am having a lovely time. A joyous heart always, **Dame Edna** 🌼

The blow has begun to fall. Putting it like that does not at first make sense, but I can explain. It's my beech trees, the most important things in my life - which they shouldn't be, I know. I probably deserve to lose them, but the thought doesn't make it any easier. Even if I deserve to lose them I can hardly think that the creatures that live in them deserve to be unhoused, and so rudely at that. I would have defended those trees with my life if anyone had attacked them, and now I have to listen to them squealing and groaning in the least wind, in their death agony.

When the road improvements were announced, I was told that our road would go under the new raised section of the M11-A11, or whatever they are going to call it, 'Royal Divorce Way' probably. That means that they will have to make a cutting that begins right on the corner of my land, well within the span of my beeches. I called every kind of lobbyist, including green ones. It was universally agreed that full-grown beech trees are extremely intolerant of root disturbance. If the excavation disturbed the drainage or the roots,the trees would give up.

I wrote to the engineers and got back the kind of 'there, there dear' letter that is reserved for fifty-three-year-old housewives. So I wrote again, pointing out that I could do without their reassurances. What I wanted was an account of the measures they were about to take to see that the survival of the trees was assured. No, I did not want to be offered compensation if they died. Yes, I was prepared to insure them, but how does an adjuster calculate the replacement cost of a hundred-foot beech or three? Who would compensate the rest of the inhabitants of my corner of Essex for the loss of their majestic presence? Could we take out insurance for a few billion or so?

On land like mine, where no other trees can find sufficient nutrients, only the beech grows so tall and full, dominating the skyline and the landscape for miles, whether showing its great dome of arching tracery in winter, or the shimmer of its trembling two-tone leaves in summer or the rich beechen brown of autumn. My beech trees are - were - the best this land can do. Everything else in my garden is mere doilies compared to the splendour of my beeches. They had stood up behind my house like sentinels; they were the last things I saw when I

Germaine Greer
Stump Cross Roundabout

went away and the first things I caught sight of when I came home. Now I cannot bear the sight of them.

I thought they had survived the hurricane of 1987. It was days later that I looked out of my study window and saw that the backyard was full of tree. A huge bough had broken off the biggest beech and clawed off more boughs from the next-door tree as it fell slowly towards the earth. I had heard nothing. The middle had fallen out of their silhouette, but still they seemed full and proud. Looking up I could see that debris in their tight forks had rotted as they grew around it, but, the rotten bough gone, they would last me out, I reckoned. I had had the tree surgeons to them, hadn't I? The surgeons had said that unlike all my other trees the beeches were fine, but of course they weren't.

I noticed that the rain seemed to make long streaks down their trunks as if it was running through deep fissures that, though barely a hair's breadth, ran from ground to crown. When I gardened near the beeches I could hear them sighing and groaning. Sometimes from quite far away I would hear a shrill crack, but the trees seemed no different afterwards.

They budded each year, but the amount of dead wood seemed to be increasing. Too many twigs fell, day in, day out. I called a different tree surgeon.

'Oh yes,' he said. 'They want taking down. They're very old after all. Can't last forever, none of us!' The notion filled him with toothy merriment, or perhaps it was just the idea of his huge fee. 'We'll cart it away for you,' he said, 'or we could leave it. Costs more if we leave it, a'course.' A'course.

'There is a preservation order on them,'I said coldly.

'Ah well, that would be a problem. But they're dangerous as they are,' he said. Could they be braced? Nothing to brace them to. Why, to each other. Well, no, because they were in a line. And the trunks are split. And he pointed to the damp sign of the treacherous rain creeping and crawling through the fault, rotting away the wood. They could have been braced when they first split, he thought, but who knew when that might have been? Certainly not I. It was too late now. The saddest words in the language. Too late. Though I had planted a new cherry laurel hedge underneath them and had a handsome new fence put up,

ILLUSTRATION BY JOHN O'CONNOR

I did not fell the beeches. It seemed to me that every month they lived was worth the risk, but gradually their beauty ebbed away. If the drought would only break, I thought, if the terrible stress on all our trees could give way to mild and sodden weather.

The drought went on. This year the spring was merciless. The beech leaves were little bigger than my thumbnail. The leaves of my horsechestnut are no bigger than my hand and every one has its edges scorched copper. The rain that is falling now serves only to rot the damaged foliage.

Some past lover of my beeches sank pipes into the ground near their boles so that a hosepipe could feed water through into their root run. They are too big now to be helped much by such devices and besides, we are subject to a drought order, phase one. Though we can use a hosepipe if we have fish or horses or swimming pools, the use of a hosepipe to save a tree is banned.

Until I got my drought order I had not realized that people consider trees less worthwhile than fish. I may not use a hosepipe to ease the stress of my young apple trees because my orchard is a tree museum and not commercial. I may not use a hosepipe to water any plant, but I can use it to clean my patio or driveway. I obey, but I do not understand.

The equinoctial winds have begun to blow. Shelley may have loved the wild west wind, breath of autumn's being and all that, and I would too, if it were not for my beeches. On two mornings now the backyard has been full of tree. The cherry laurel hedge is crushed and the new fence is hanging tipsily. My trees are coming down, crazily, perilously down. Two thirds of their crowns are down already. When the night wind pulls at the remaining branches, their sighs and groans become cracks and screams. By day the stubs of broken boughs gore the dirty sky. I should have got the permission to fell the beeches, should have committed euthanasia. I walk along the hedge and count the self-seeded baby beeches. I shall not last long enough to see them come waist high to my old trees. The scruffy lime-tree that skulks under them on one side, even if it conquers pollution and chalk and wind, will never beat its own woolly aphids. The road-builders and the Water Board have got it right after all. It is wrong to be breaking my heart over three silly old trees. 🍂

'Are you sure there isn't, Edith?'

'Go on without me – save yourself!'

Interview

John Mortimer

The writer barrister and 'committed leftie' talks to *Naim Attallah*
about lawyers, politics and the birth of Rumpole of the Bailey

Yours was the sort of childhood that, had you grown up into a complete neurotic or developed almost any other kind of psychosis, it would have been entirely explicable in terms of your early years. How on earth did you turn out to be so normal?

It's a question whether I am normal at all. In many ways, however, I had a very happy childhood because I had a father and mother who treated me very well and always as though I was grown up. And I was an only child which has its advantages, in that you grow up very quickly. I was treated like a good friend, especially by my father. He flew into terrible rages with other people but never with me, and my mother was long-suffering and loving.

Both your parents were adept at not acknowledging reality. Your father did not admit to his blindness and your mother, long after his death, continued to behave as if he had not died. The making light of sorrow and grief is something quintessentially English. Is it something you have inherited?

There is a wonderful story about Lord Uxbridge whose leg was shot off at the Battle of Waterloo, and when the Duke of Wellington said, 'By God, Uxbridge, you've lost your leg!', Lord Uxbridge looked down and said, 'By God, Sir, so I have!' And nothing more was said. But that isn't altogether a failure to accept reality– it's more a stoical attitude to life which I think is quite admirable. Whether it's courage or a refusal to face facts, I'm not quite sure, but that's how I prefer to live. I can quite easily put unpleasant facts out of my head – I don't think about death for instance.

You have often said that you believe in middle-class virtues. Can you explain to me what these are?

SALLY AND RICHARD GREENHILL / ALAMY STOCK PHOTO

They are really the virtues I saw in my mother and father. To begin with, it wasn't anything to do with money. They were both liberal, my mother a sort of Shavian new woman, my father an old-fashioned Lloyd George Liberal. They were professional people, my father especially in the sense that he gave very good advice to the clients he was acting for. He didn't think about doing it for the money, though he liked being paid. In those days barristers often did cases for nothing and I certainly started that way. There was a kind of tradition of middle class professionalism, of tolerance, liberalism, all of those things, which I admire. The middle classes have been the source of most of the strength of England, and most writers have come from the middle class. With the exception of Byron and Shelley, the aristocracy haven't produced many writers, and working-class traditions have tended to keep people in rather stereotyped conditions of mind. Political change also has come mainly from the middle classes, and all the best revolutionaries have been middle class.

There is a character in *Paradise Postponed* who is in favour of the working classes running the country while at the same time doubting if these were the kind of people she would have to tea. Does that perhaps epitomise the dichotomy in your own attitude towards the working class?

In *Paradise Postponed* I wanted to be as rude about my side as I was about the other side. I was getting at a type of left-wing person, particularly of that era of the Webbs, Virginia Woolf, Leonard Woolf and those sort of people, who managed to combine the view that the working classes should take over the world, with the feeling that they themselves, being extremely privileged Bloomsbury persons, wouldn't have them to tea. But I don't honestly think that that's my own attitude. I'm as sceptical about liberal left-wing policies as I am about everything else. The radio quarrel with Julie Burchill when she accused me of being a snob made me think very closely about whether I am one, but I honestly don't think so.

Your fellow barrister Geoffrey Robertson said of you: 'There is a legal part of John Mortimer's work which is deeply conservative, deeply rooted in the law.' Do you think that was the case when you practised?

It is absolutely true to say there is a part of me that is deeply conservative – I want the countryside to be kept as it is, I don't want the English landscape to change, and I want English country life to be kept as it is. I'm also very conservative about the British constitution, which I think works well, and about the British system of justice. My whole attitude towards being a barrister is that the law is a kind of disease and you should try and cure your clients of it as quickly as possible.

You married for the first time when you were 26 and inherited a ready-made family of four children. After the solitude of your own childhood, did the prospect of a large family attract you?

I think it did. I was really entranced by the idea of a lot of children and since then I've never lived without children around. I have children now of all possible ages, from 42 to eight years old.

Since your wife had first to secure a divorce before you could be married, you went to considerable lengths to be cited as co-respondent. One imagines that in those days it was rather a sordid business with a great deal of stigma attached to it ...

We used to go to endless numbers of hotels and try to make people remember we'd been there. No one ever did, but in the end a private detective called Mr Smith came to the house and found our clothes in the same bedroom, and then I made a confession. Mr Smith later gave evidence in court that we were living together. The following week I was conducting my first case as a barrister and I had to call this same Mr Smith as a witness to the adultery of the people whose case I was handling. For the next 30 years I called Mr Smith to testify about once a week. One day Mr Smith was walking across a pedestrian crossing and a police car came buzzing along and nearly ran him over, so he hit the police car on the roof in a fit of anger, whereupon the policeman arrested him. Mr Smith sued the police for false arrest. I went to court and said I'd known Mr Smith for 30 years and he was an absolutely truthful, honest character. He got substantial damages.

'The great advantage of old age is that you can behave quite childishly, whereas when you're young you're very anxious to appear grown up'

Your marriage to the first Penelope was legendary in its tempestuousness. Most people find perpetual fighting draining and debilitating, yet you continued to work hard and write hard. Did you perhaps find a certain exhilaration or energy in the conflict?

Not really. I had £5 a week from my father, four children to feed, a very large house in Hampstead, and another house somebody gave us in the countryside. So I really had to work. I not only earned money by divorcing people, but I wrote anything – stories for women's magazines, anything. Two writers married to each other is an impossible situation, because you're using the same material and using each other's lives. It was certainly tempestuous, but it gave us both a lot of material, and it wasn't without moments of happiness. When I look back on it now, however, I can't think how I survived it. I must have had enormous stamina.

After the breakdown of your first marriage you had two promiscuous years. Were those the years you should have had before you were married perhaps?

Absolutely. I became middle-aged quite early on, and then I had to go back to being young again. I didn't go totally mad, but I was always on the lookout. I think I'm naturally somebody who wants to live with a family and children, and I wouldn't now like to have to embark at my age on a promiscuous period. I think it would be very exhausting.

You used to say that when you grew up you would decide between being a writer and a barrister. Since you have left the bar, does that mean you have finally grown up?

A good question. I didn't decide for years and years to leave the Bar, and I think I left it about ten years too late. The great advantage of old age is that you can behave quite childishly, whereas when you're young you're very anxious to appear grown up. I always was a writer who did a bit of barristering. I still don't know whether I've finally grown up ...

You claim always to have felt somewhat out of place at the Bar. Why was that?

When I started everybody was frightfully correct and conservative, and called each other by their surnames, as though they were still at prep school; and there was I, rather left-wing, writing plays, going off at the end of a court to go to rehearsals and take actresses out. So I was slightly out of place, though not completely, because I had of course been a child round the Temple.

You grew up in an agnostic household and have never been able to bring yourself to believe in God. Have you ever felt that as a particular loss?

I wasn't ever christened or confirmed, so I grew up with no religion, but I never missed it at all. And I always admired my father, because although he went blind and had awful things happen to him, he never turned to God. But I am very interested in religion – I think sometimes atheists become obsessed with religion, and I certainly love talking to bishops, or arguing with cardinals. My problem with religion, or with an omnipotent deity, is to see why he puts up with all the evil in the world. I can't work it out and I can't work out whether I would like God if he existed. There have been more horrible deeds perpetrated in the name of religion than for anything else, and it's difficult ☞

Leo McKern, in costume, with Mortimer for an episode of *Rumpole*

not to believe that the religions of the world have done more harm than good. As a writer, however, I am aware that Catholicism has provided a wonderful kind of starting-off point for novelists. If you're Graham Greene or Evelyn Waugh you can have a kind of framework for your life and your writing which I don't have, and which I suppose I might envy.

But as you get older don't you hanker after some sort of faith?
No, I don't, honestly. And I certainly don't hanker after immortality.

You have often been criticised for being a 'champagne socialist' and have defended yourself by claiming your role was to infiltrate the Establishment in order to change it. Do you think you can claim success in that respect?
I just believe champagne should be freely available to all. Nye Bevan was forever drinking champagne, and that was a very good sign. I also don't think attacking the Establishment from the outside has much effect. The best form of attack is humour. If you get the jury to laugh in court you know you've won the case.

Beneath your own cheerfulness and bonhomie, I suspect there is a grim pessimism, and malaise ...
Pessimism is a very good basis for a cheerful outlook on life. If you don't expect too much you won't be disappointed. I always used to tell my clients that they could go to prison for six years, and when they ended up by being fined £2 they were frightfully relieved. But if you told them they were going to be fined ten shillings and they were fined £2, they would have been very cross. It is better to expect the worst.

Your preferred genre for writing is comedy. Do you think that is the best way of saying important things, or is there perhaps a danger that important issues will be seen to be trivialised?
That's a very good question. Comedy is the most important and the most difficult form of writing. It's a great English tradition, from the comedies of Shakespeare such as *Twelfth Night* and *As You Like It*, which are quite sad plays really, through to the novels of Dickens, which can be tragic and comic and savage at the same time. Comedy is also the most truthful thing – if you rule out comedy you rule out half of the truth. Does it trivialise the truth? I don't think it does. Quite the reverse.

You are very sensitive to criticism and unfavourable reviews. Haven't you reached a stage where you can afford to ignore adverse comments?
I've now stopped reading reviews. They are just quite irritating and it can be bad for the confidence. Dickens never read reviews, then suddenly he read a bad review of *Little Dorrit* by mistake and got into a terrible depression.

There are many contradictions in your character. Have you ever tried to resolve these contradictions?
Oh no, I wouldn't like to resolve them. I would cease to exist if I did that. Contradictions are essential – if

you're writing, you have to have the tension, which is the different parts of your character.

I have the impression that being unable to get close to your mother, even at the end of her life, was one of the hardest and saddest things for you ...
Yes, it's one of my greatest regrets. I think because I had a very strong relationship with my father, she was rather left out. Also she came from the English tradition of not being demonstrative. Her father committed suicide and while she was in South Africa her family just sent her the local paper with a note saying: 'This story will probably interest you'. As a family they didn't talk about anything like that. And although we weren't quite so remote, it was never as close as I should have liked.

Looking back on your life, what are you proudest of?
Of the good things I have written, *Clinging to the Wreckage*, *Voyage Round My Father*, and I'm also rather proud of *Rumpole*. It's quite difficult for a writer to keep going in a lot of different generations, and I'm pleased to have done that. I'm proud of my children, and happy to have kept my parents' house in the condition it's been accustomed to. I don't think my achievements have been really great. I hope I've been on the side of tolerance, liberalism, letting people alone and social justice, but millions of people have said all those things, so it's not anything I feel particularly responsible for.

You have sometimes said that to conduct an interview is much more difficult than to be interviewed... Do you still take that view?
This has been such a good interview that it's made me think very deeply. I was never quite so well prepared as you, and it is always nerve-racking until the interviewee suddenly says something extraordinary and then you can relax in the knowledge you've got the whole thing wrapped up. I remember interviewing Lord Hailsham and asking him what he did when he sat on the Woolsack looking bored. And he said, 'I whisper "bollocks" to the bench of bishops'. And I knew that since I had got him to say that, everything would be all right. ◍

'Dad, why do they call us "Travellers"?'

The art of Kathleen Hale, creator of Orlando the Marmalade Cat, has delighted generations of children. *Merlin Holland* asks her how she cast her magic spell

A Toast to the Marmalade Cat

We first met 40 years ago when I was about eight and she in her mid-fifties. On reflection it was grossly ill-mannered of me to have refused a kiss to one who had already given me so much youthful pleasure, but independence is important at that age and father's old friend or no, I wasn't having any of it. I must have been forgiven, though, for she signed all my wellthumbed Orlando books and sent me a copy of *A Seaside Holiday* a year later 'with love from Orlando, Grace, Pansy, Blanche and Tinkle'.

Thirty years went by, I had a young family of my own and the world seemed to have been taken over, triffid-like, by *Mr Men*. I turned in despair to the books of my childhood, *Orlando* amongst others, but I was quite unready for the electric effect which the centre-page spread of *Orlando Buys a Farm* would have on dormant memories. My own reaction aside, their introduction to a new generation was a triumph. 'The pictures are so big I can climb into them,' said my son, faced with pages half his own height. 'That,' explained Kathleen Hale, 'is exactly what I had intended.'

Bringing up her own family in 1934, she was equally frustrated by the lack of imaginative children's books and took to inventing stories to keep them amused. Some time later she complained of the problem to an old friend and editor of

the *Cambridge Magazine*, CK Ogden. He offered to translate her tales and include them in a series of pocket books he was publishing for children in Japan if she would write them down with illustrations in black and white. For Kathleen, who had been earning a living as an artist since 1918, the constraints of size and lack of colour were impossible

Above: Kathleen Hale at home in Oxfordshire. Left: in 1967, my father told Kathleen he had seen himself on colour TV in America. She drew this sketch for him

conditions. She knew how children loved large books from watching two or three of them lie on the floor and share *Babar the Elephant*, so she wrote Orlando's Camping Holiday and *Orlando's Trip Abroad*, illustrated in seven colours and designed as foliosized volumes.

For two years her agent tried in vain to place them. Finally *Country Life* agreed to publish but insisted that the printers' in-house lithographer redraw the illustrations so that they could be reproduced as a combination of the four standard printing colours - red, yellow, blue and black. It was a proceedure similar to the professional engravers of the 18th and 19th centuries reducing portraits to printable size - competent reproduction, but somehow lacking the spontaneity of the original. It also answers the nagging question of why I never quite loved the cats in *A Camping Holiday* as much as I did in all the later books - they weren't yet entirely Kathleen Hale.

From then on she insisted on doing her own lithographic work. The printer would deliver huge zinc plates, the size of four finished pages, and she would draw her illustrations directly on to them, one for each of the three primary colours and black. Easy enough if you can see the finished drawing, but unimaginably difficult if you are working with black litho chalks on a grey surface and having to make up the colours in your mind, all the time keeping them in register. Later the printers developed fine sheets of transparent plastic with a roughened surface which helped with the register, but she still needed to work with black chalks and imagine the colour combinations she was creating. The process wasn't helped by the chalks which were made of wax and softened unmanageably in warm weather. Keeping them in the fridge was partially successful, but in the end she was limited to working in autumn and winter.

When I first went to see Kathleen about the *Orlando* books last autumn, I was expecting to find a dreamy, rather fey woman in her early eighties. Instead I was faced with an astoundingly alert ninety-five year old, with a sharp wit and an impish sense of humour who had just written her autobiography. Her father had died, heavily in debt, when she was only five, leaving her mother to fend for the three children. Kathleen was farmed out to grandparents and an aunt before the family was reunited in Manchester when she was nine. It was an unsettling time. Was the idealised cat-family life of the books an attempt to recreate what she had missed in those years?

'Of course. And by the middle of the war when five had already been published I was always hoping that the evacuee children would be helped by them. They must have felt very much as I did separated from their parents.' Unexpectedly, though, Pansy, Blanche and Tinkle were not simply herself, her sister and her brother. 'No, Tinkle was me. It was a much softened and more charming me. I was a complete rebel against the smug respectability of Didsbury where we lived. I refused to do my lessons at school and spent most of my nine years there in the corridor in disgrace. But I lived for my drawing and the worst punishment my mother could give me was to take away my drawing things. Once I was nearly expelled for drawing bare-breasted mermaids round the margins of my scripture book but the headmistress overlooked it.' The same headmistress recognised Kathleen's ability and entered her for an art scholarship at Reading University College, which, to the annoyance of her contemporaries, 'the worst girl in the school' won.

After art school she came to London and joined the land-army in 1918, driving heavy horses from Barnes to

An unpublished watercolour of Orlando

Covent Garden daily. More material for the *Orlando* books, as it later turned out. Living on a shoestring in London she became part of the 1920s bohemia, somehow floating along on the lifebuoy of her remarkable talent. A chance meeting and a moment's banter with Augustus John landed her a job as his assistant and a long friendship.

Until recently, like most people, I was quite unaware of the outstanding quality of her other work. Some of the best is reproduced in her book. Did she feel any regrets that she had hung her 'slender reputation on the broad shoulders of a eunuch cat', as her friend Cedric Morris once put it? 'Those cats! Once I had done

two books they became so real to me that they were in charge. I had a certain amount of control over them but they were always escaping. I would like to be remembered for my serious work but somehow Orlando took over.'

Well, Kathleen, it should be some consolation to know that you've given such pleasure to thousands of children over two generations and you've evened up the imbalance in that autobiography - essential reading for all Orlando lovers. Have a very happy ninety-sixth on the 24th May. ◑

Kathleen Hale: 24th May 1898- 26th January 2000

Rage
Auberon Waugh

Physicians have traditionally been allowed a certain licence to bump off hopeless oldies

It is now more or less officially accepted that the *Times* was lying when it reported on January 21st, 1936 that King George V's last words on earth, uttered the previous night, had been, 'How is the Empire?' Mr Francis Oppier, thirty-one-year-old Mayor of Bognor Regis, the ghastly Sussex resort, now wishes the alternative version to be accepted - that the King, on being assured he was getting better and would soon be sent to Bognor Regis to recuperate, replied 'Bugger Bognor', and those were his last words.

In a world where Bognor has mayors of thirty-one, some such decision was inevitable. Perhaps they will stick the words in letters of gold over the town hall: 'Bognor is the venue for the annual Clown Convention and the Birdman Rally where hundreds of people jump off the pier, so we know how to have a bit of fun,' says Oppier. 'Anyway, any publicity is good publicity.' If King George really said 'Bugger Bognor' as he lay dying at the age of seventy, it was just about the only occasion on which he might be said to have thrown over the Royal traces. It was also the only occasion on which he heeded the sentiment, which inspires this column and gives it its name, in Dylan Thomas's lines:

'Do not go gentle into that good night Rage, rage against the dying of the light.'

If the King's expletive was intended to show resistance to inexorable fate, it did him no good. Even as the words left his lips, Lord Dawson of Penn, physician-in-ordinary to four English kings, was striding towards the King's bedroom in Sandringham to deliver the fatal injection of morphine into his jugular artery which would send him on his way like a lamb. As Lord Dawson explained to his Diary, it was necessary for the King to die after the last editions of the evening newspapers but in good time for the first edition of the *Times*, which would carry the mendacious news to the three corners of the earth that King George V had died asking about the Empire.

There can be no doubt that by the law of the land, then as now, Lord Dawson had committed murder, for which the penalty was then death by hanging. In fact, I believe he could still be hanged for what he did, since regicide comes under

the general heading of treason, which still carries the death penalty. Instead of which, a grateful King Edward VIII rewarded him by promoting him from baron to viscount, (these distinctions still counted, in those days), and he went on to be physicianin-ordinary to a two further monarchs, dying, covered in honours, at the age of eighty-one, in 1945.

The greatest difference between Dawson and Dr Nigel Cox, the Winchester hospital consultant up before the Bench recently for despatching an old lady who was incurably ill and in great pain, is that Dawson knew how these things should be done. Although I have never heard of anyone injecting morphine into the jugular artery as an analgesic measure - or, for that matter, injecting anything into the jugular artery for any purpose - the fact remains that morphine (like heroin) is used primarily as a pain-killer,

whereas potassium chloride, which Dr Cox used to kill Lillian Boyes, is not.

At forty-seven, Dr Cox is old enough to grasp the philosophical distinction between primary intention and secondary effect. It is on the doctrine of secondary effect that physicians have traditionally been allowed a certain licence to bump off hopeless oldies. Both morphine and heroin are pain-killers as well as powerful poisons, but with repeated use, the body acquires an immunity until the only effective analgesic is also a lethal overdose. There you can reasonably say that the primary purpose of the injection is to reduce pain, even with death as a necessary side-effect. When Dr Cox's counsel argued that his primary intention in injecting a massive overdose of potassium chloride had been to alleviate her suffering, and not to kill her, he must have been wrong since potassium chloride has no analgesic function. It merely influences the activity of the heart - in Dr Cox's dosage, stopping it.

All this may seem somewhat jesuitical, and a bad advertisement for a Catholic education, but we must remember that if Dr Cox had been charged with murder rather than attempted murder (as he could easily have been charged, in the light of Mrs Boyes' death a few minutes later), the statutory minimum sentence would have been life. The overall effect of Dr Cox's prosecution has been to create an outcry for the liberalizing of the law on euthanasia, and since none of us wishes to linger in a pain-wracked, helpless state, it would be easy to join in.

But there is something more than casuistry in the distinction between administering an analgesic drug whose secondary effect is lethal, and de-livering a lethal drug whose secondary effect is (inevitably) to put an end to discomfort. The difference is between doing things properly and not doing them properly. This may seem unimportant when discussing matters of life and death, but if doctors are allowed to run a slack ship, it will be the same slack ship which they take into the waters of any new, more permissive legislation on the subject. As we grow older, we must remember that however much we wish to avoid a painful or undignified and lingering death, there is a hungry, impatient and largely amoral younger generation waiting for us to move on. ◖

'Before we start, why don't we go round and each say a little something about ourselves?'

BILL PROUD

My class war

James Pembroke sets out to prove that 'Business Manager* of The Oldie' is the grandest title he could ever claim

'**P**oshy' is my least favourite nickname – 'Fatty' was far better. At school, at least I could feel that the latter was a temporary burden from which strict dieting would release me.

'Poshy', dealt to me by my last workmates at *City Limits*, a hard-left magazine, and then taken on with some glee by *The Oldie*'s Editor, was much harder to shift. Enter my inadvertent rescuer: the Hon Ursula Wyndham.

Traditionally, one's ancestry has not been a topic of conversation among the English. Either they know nothing at all about their forefathers and don't care, or they know things they wish they didn't and claim they don't care, or they say they are not remotely interested, but hint that Debrett's would provide the answer.

As a result, genealogists have generally been accorded the same degree of resect as trainspotters.

Until recently, I knew very little about my forebears, but I was fond of a dubious family myth that we were descended from an orphan who was adopted by the Earl of Pembroke. Apparently, it was ☞

> **Traditionally, one's ancestry has not been a topic of conversation among the English**

TEA?

OFFER ENDS SOON

ROBERT THOMPSON

fashionable in the late 18th century for the aristocracy to adopt orphans by the boatload and give them the family name, rather in the way one can adopt aardvarks in London Zoo today.

The only other time I had become interested in my family was on my 16th birthday. My mother took some of my friends and me out to lunch and told us all that I was related to someone famous called David Gilmore. 'Not Dave Gilmore of Pink Floyd?!' they cried. My credibility soared as a result of my close ties to pop glory, and over the next two years, Dave Gilmore gradually rose from being my fourth cousin to being my first.

That particular balloon finally burst a year ago when someone came up to my wife and me at a concert and asked if we wanted to meet Dave Gilmore. 'Of course,' said my wife. 'He's James's cousin.' I begged not to meet him but was duly dragged to the pop star's door. I was introduced to him as his cousin. 'Oh yeah?' he growled. 'What's your name?' 'Well, Pembroke,' I spluttered.

'You see, my grandmother on my mother's side and your grandmother on your father's ...' 'Piss off,' said cousin Dave.

I had learnt my lesson. I never wanted to dabble in family history again. So when, at an *Oldie* editorial lunch, Ursula Wyndham discovered my name was Pembroke, and mistakenly but excitedly announced to the entire table that she was sitting next to the Earl of Pembroke, I squirmed again.

After two hours I thought I had convinced her that I wasn't the Earl, having duly trotted out my implausible story about orphans. Ursula would have none of it. As far as she was concerned I was of noble blood. She promptly returned home and contacted Wilton House, the Pembroke family pile, and repeated the whole story to the aged dowager countess. Still unsatisfied, she contacted the Wiltshire County records office, and discovered that the 10th Earl, who lived in the 1790s, fathered several illegitimate children and his wife had indeed provided for them. There was no evidence that their surname was Pembroke, but Ursula was convinced. She had also discovered that she was distantly related to the Earls of Pembroke, and three notes followed in quick succession, addressed to 'Cousin James', demanding that I admit to my

'My grandmother on my mother's side and your grandmother on your father's ...' 'Piss off,' said cousin Dave

newly acquired lineage. One of her missives was most emphatic: 'I admit it's no pleasure being descended from the Herberts [the Earl's family name], but surely it's better than springing from nowhere! Come on. Be a man and face up to it. I shall not stop looking on you as a long-lost cousin.'

I still couldn't feel any blue blood trickling through my veins, but the name 'Poshy' had now stuck firmly with the *Oldie* staff. I was getting increasingly fed up with it, and was desperately advocating the poor orphan alternative to a friend, hoping someone would accept my man-of-the-people credentials. Suddenly she became very animated. Yes, yes, she was reading a book and it was absolutely true that on 29th March 1741, 30 members of the aristocracy had adopted some orphans in the good care of Thomas Coram, at the Foundling Hospital. The Countess of Pembroke was indeed one of these blue-bloods and, following the example of others, she gave the name Pembroke to her orphan. I became determined to establish the truth. Ursula remained immoveable, and so the Editor suggested that I engage a firm of forebear-sleuths to convince her once and for all.

I duly contacted Windsor Ancestry Research and told them the whole story. I explained that the point of my quest, as opposed to the normal aspirations of their clients, was to prove that I was *not* related to the Earls of Pembroke, on either side of the sheets. My real hope was that I would be related to the Pembroke orphan.

I had imagined that the research would be a simple process. Sadly, not. The first census of the population of England and Wales was in 1801, and until 1851 these censuses acted as little more

than a headcount for tax purposes. From 1851 onwards the censuses give a more detailed description of the population, including their precise ages and places of birth.

Within a week, I received the birth certificate of my great-grandfather, Sydney, who was born in 1857. It also gave the name and occupation of his father. It looked as though the game was going to be up for Ursula. Our Sid's Dad, William Pembroke, was a butcher, albeit a master butcher, in the Old Kent Road.

Next we had to establish William's forefathers. Fortunately, William had married in 1851, the year of the first proper census, and his marriage certificate shows that both his father and father-in-law were butchers. This was getting better and better. However, going any further back and finding William's father's birth certificate, and hence the identity of William's grandfather, was going to be far more tricky. He would have been born about the same time as the Pembroke-adopted orphan.

The main sources for ancestry research prior to the beginning of civil registration are the parish registers, so you have to know which parish your last known ancestor lived in. The nearest approach to a comprehensive index to English parish registers is the International Genealogical Index, which lists many of the parish entries for baptisms and marriages. The distinctly low-rent demesne of Deptford, not Wilton, came up with a long line of William Pembrokes. Sid's dad, William (born 1823) was the son of William and Sarah. And that William (born 1774) was the son of William and Hannah. And that William was born in 1743, the son of William and Mary. In other words, I couldn't possibly be descended from Thomas Coram's orphan.

I must admit to missing him. But at least I had knocked Ursula's skew-whiff coronet off my plebeian brow. My uncle dealt the final blow. He said that he had known all along about the Deptford Pembrokes; that they were sea captains, probably slavers; that there was nothing wrong with butchers; and that I was a frightful snob to think we were ever anything else. But the Editor still insists on calling me 'Poshy'. ◍

James has since risen to the dizzying heights of publisher of The Oldie

SAMSUNG Galaxy Tab A8
easology

The latest spec tablet simplifed for you...

The Samsung Galaxy Tab A8 Easology has been specially designed for ease-of-use, yet it is also packed with the very latest technology and features...

Technology is central to our lives, yet are you sometimes left wondering why it cannot be easier? That's where the Samsung Galaxy Tab A8 easology comes in....

We identified ways that tablets can be made easier-to-use. From simple changes like larger text and bigger icons, to more involved understanding of how people use their tablet. In a ground-breaking collaboration with Samsung, we have developed an interface that's easy-to-use, allowing you to access the word-class functionality that Samsung offer in their tablets.

Easy-To-Use
Designed with ease in mind, this Samsung easology tablet makes the latest technology available to all. Find clearer layouts, easy internet browsing, larger text, big icons and much more.

Stylish, Sleek And Powerful
The Samsung Galaxy Tab A8 easology is perfect for searching the internet, video calls, watching videos, social media and more.

Only £229.99
With FREE Delivery

FREE stylish case
while stocks last

The Samsung Galaxy Tab A8 Easology is just so simple to use...

EASY SEARCHING
Internet browser with buttons to magnify.

EASY READING
Easier reading with large text.

DOWNLOAD APPS
Download your favourite apps.

EASY FEATURES
A magnifier for reading instructions.

EASY LAYOUTS
Enjoy intuitive screen layouts.

EASY NAVIGATION
Clear actions and buttons.

A8 TABLET SPECIFICATIONS   WiFi

- Easy-to-use interface
- Large 10.5" HD screen
- 32GB storage
- WiFi connection
- All-day battery
- Front and rear cameras
- Add storage with a microSD card

The easology home screen explained
The home screen is split into 4 main sections:

A Features the time, date and weather for your area.

B A list of your favourite apps. Download apps from the Google Play Store and add them to your home screen.

C A row of apps you are likely to use the most, including a handy magnifier, camera, settings and internet.

D Four quick contacts you can assign to friends and family, or anyone you might need to contact easily.

E The home button. A single tap on this rounded square will return you to the familiarity of the home screen at any time.

▶ Watch online at www.easology.net/a8

Don't just take our word for it...

❝ I am very happy with my new Samsung easology tablet. It is nice and easy to use. I am very happy with the purchase and can 100% recommend." Jenny, 71, Cardiff
★★★★★

"I have been online for 20 years and wanted a new tablet with the latest technology. My Samsung easology has a great screen, great sound and is fast. It's also really easy-to-use. Being online has never been so enjoyable!" ❞ Gerry, 76, Cleveland
★★★★★

ORDER BY PHONE (Local Rate)
0118 418 1217
08:30 - 20:00 Mon-Fri. 9:00 - 14:00 Sat.

ORDER ONLINE
www.easology.net

 Free Delivery
 2-Year Warranty
 Secure Payment

Summer people

A short story by *D J Taylor*

The Summer People began arriving in May. They came in small, rickety trains on the branch line from Cromer, in smoking cars, or were disgorged from charabancs and coaches in the marketplace. From his vantage point at an upstairs window Julian watched them toil to the crest of the hill, where the rows of holiday cottages began: framed by his moving hand they re-emerged as perspiring, red-faced men awkwardly manhandling cases, children in the skimpy clothing their parents had thought suitable for a Norfolk summer, frozen by the wind. There was a pattern to their migrations. May brought young, childless couples who loitered hand-in-hand along the front or turned over the bric-a-brac in the sixpenny arcade. In July came holidaying families who foraged over the rock-pools for crabs and crayfish; in late August a few pensioners who drowsed in the end-of-season sun. By September the town had reverted to its antique state: rain falling over the pebbledash houses, sending the high street shoppers scurrying for cover beneath awnings or into the porch of St Peter's Church. In the distance cloud hung over the long grey spar of the sea.

As the town's second-largest newsagent-cum-stationer, Mr Holroyd could not afford to despise the Summer People, but he allowed himself sardonic remarks over their choice of newspaper - which, for example, preferred the *Guardian* to the *Times* or the *Daily Telegraph*, or declined to place sixpences in the box held up by the imploring blind boy. Once, in distant days, a man had requested the *Morning Star*. Mr Holroyd had pushed it with his own hands through the narrow holiday-home letterbox, so great was his disgust. The Summer People irked Mr Holroyd. He disliked their grainy Midlands accents, the too-easily earned five pound notes picked up in the engineering shops of Wolverhampton and Dudley which they flicked over the counter in exchange for cigarettes and ice-cream, and he

suspected them of sexual irregularity, or what passed for sexual irregularity in Sheringham in the 1960s. But he made an exception of Miss Hoare, who arrived in the town halfway through July, rented an expensive property on the cliff and spent 50 shillings on sketching pads on her first visit to the shop.

'A very personable woman,' he informed the silent breakfast table audience of wife and son. 'She was staying at the Saracen's Head, but apparently the light wasn't what she wanted.'

The Saracen's Head was the most expensive hotel in Sheringham. The town's masonic lodge met in its back parlour on alternate Thursdays. Mr and Mrs Holroyd occasionally took afternoon tea there in a rather ostentatious way on winter Saturdays.

Julian first caught sight of Miss Hoare two days later in the shop, where she was making a fuss about cartridge paper. She was a large, fat but undoubtedly stylish woman in early middle age, her clothes of a kind not generally seen in Sheringham: a billowing dirndl skirt, white blouse pattered with sunflowers, wide-brimmed Panama hat. Stepping suddenly from the street into the cool interior, Julian heard her say: 'Of course the A4 is no good at all. Would it be possible to get the A3, do you think?' Unexpectedly, Julian heard his mother agreeing to this request: similar demands, made by sun-cured old men for obscure angling magazines, had not been so kindly received. 'This is Julian,' she said in a slightly subdued way, as he moved further into the shop towards the counter. Miss Hoare gave him a frank, appraising stare of the kind that old farmers at the County Show bestowed on horses. 'Oh yes,' she said. 'You're the young man who's so keen on art,· and Julian smiled wretchedly, not wanting his private experiments with watercolours and charcoal to be known to a pale-faced woman of forty with cropped hair and scarlet lipstick. 'I'll call again then, about the paper.· Miss Hoare said briskly to his mother, gathering up a little pile of purchases that included three packets of Park Drive cigarette and a sophisticated women's magazine in which Mrs Holroyd made occasional scandalised forays.

When she had gone, mother and son sat on the low stools behind the counter in a space made smaller by her absence, as motes of dust danced in the sulight of

the open door and shadow fell over the rows of shrimping nets and water pistols. Eventually the silence was broken by a gang of children squabbling over the ice-cream chiller. 'I except we can get the cartridge paper from Norwich,' Mrs Holroyd said vaguely. 'She needs it for her work, you see ... ' Mrs Holroyd added as an afterthought: 'That lipstick ... '

It was a hot summer that year. Julian drew salmon-skinned children who romped on the worm-casted sand beneath the pier, or shrieked at the Punch and Judy, old fat women swimming sedately like porpoises in the shallows. Mrs Holroyd chided him affectionately, small things and large things mixed: the condition of his room, the length of his hair, his self-absorption. Impending O level results, she implied, were no excuse for sequestration. In the end he embarked on long, futile cycle rides out along the north Norfolk flat, towards Wells and Blakeney. These too had their Summer People: well-groomed schoolgirls playing tennis on windswept courts overlooking the sea; civil young men in boats. Miss Hoare turned up frequently on these excursions, seated, sketch pad on knee, in rock crannies on the cliff path or arranging her easel on the beach. Occasionally she smiled or waved a hand from which cigarette smoke trickled slowly into the dense air. Once Julian found the easel unattended halfway up the stone escarpment flanking the putting course. He had time to register an enticing impressionist's vista of frothing waves and shipwrecked mariners before the sound of footsteps from below drove him away.

Each night at supper Mr Holroyd uncovered the little cache of lore which the day's traffic had afforded him. 'I asked about that Miss Hoare. At the Saracen's Head.' They ate Cromer crabs, shrimps, salad, dyspeptic hunks of white bread. Mr Holroyd was an advocate of 'plain English food': a birthday dinner had once been ruined by the intrusion of alien sauces. 'Apparently she's made quite a name for herself. Exhibitions and so on. At any rate she seems to make a living out of it.' Julian bent his head at the implied rebuke, which was, he knew, intended to emphasise the distance between an Art sanctified by commerce and feckless bohemian daydreaming. Later that evening Mrs Holroyd sought him out in a bedroom lined with neatly executed Airfix kits and pictures of the England World Cup squad. 'You mustn't mind your dad,' she said. 'He just wants what's best for you.' The letter from Julian's headmaster, pressing the claims of the sixth-form science course and stating the necessity of a speedy decision, lay on the sill next to the Collected Drawings of Aubrey Beardsley, which Mr Holroyd had looked through with tolerant disdain. 'And you could always keep up your drawing,' Mrs Holroyd suggested timorously, 'as a kind of hobby perhaps...'

Once, the summer before, Julian had disappeared on his bicycle for an entire day, returning only at dusk, an hour after Mr Holroyd had telephoned the police. 'Why did you do it?' his father had asked, shocked and puzzled out of his evening routine of checking the stock cupboard and bundling up unsold copies of the *Daily Mirror*. 'I did it to get away from you,' Julian had answered, which was honest but scarcely sensible. Memories of this incident still rankled.

The next evening his father said unexpectedly: 'I saw that Mrs Hoare the other day.' 'Yes?' 'A very interesting woman, that. Who was it she was telling me about? Some artist chap or other that she knew... Anyway, the upshot of it was that she wondered if you'd like some help with your drawing.' 'Perhaps,' Julian heard himself saying, 'she could have asked me herself.' But Mrs Holroyd was absorbed in the correspondence columns of the *Cromer Mercury*. 'I don't think there's any call for that kind of remark,' he said absently.

Julian had little experience of women in early middle age, let alone artistic ☞

ones. Mrs Arkwright, the school's art department, specialised in Norfolk landscapes populated by vast, Stubbsian horses. A spinster friend of his mother's routinely dispensed faded, self-painted watercolours as Christmas presents. Miss Hoare, etching in the corners of her tumultuous seascapes, seemed infinitely removed from these pale exemplars. She painted putting courses filled with giant golfers waving their irons like weapons, a vortex of wind, debris and flailing black birds descending on the spire of St Peter's church. 'You can be honest with me,' she told Julian. 'Do you like them?' 'I don't dislike them,' Julian replied truthfully. 'But in the sea picture you've put the gulls in the wrong place. You see, they always alight on the highest point.' Miss Hoare was delighted. 'A very good answer,' she said. 'If you'd said you liked them, I wouldn't have believed you.'

Conscious of their roles as native and interloper, they strolled around the town in search of vantage points: the gallery of the church, the high ground to the north, the tiny station with its dozing porter. 'Why Sheringham?' Julian asked at one point. 'I mean ... ' He stopped for a second, crimson-faced. 'I thought artists went to the South of France, places like that.' 'So they do,' Miss Hoare said judiciously. 'But my dear, I've had enough of Menton and Nice to last me a lifetime. Full of hopeless Englishmen thinking they're Pierre Loti.' Reaching the front again, they turned into the high street. Here the characteristie high summer smells hung in the air: fried fish, candyfloss, oil, each mixed witih the pervasive tang of salt. 'Do you suppose,' Miss Hoare wondered, 'there is anywhere we could get a drink? A proper drink, that is.' 'Not a chance,' Julian told her cheerfully. 'Everyone knows I've only just turned sixteen. If l went into a pub and ordered a half of cider they'd probably telephone my father.' 'Oh well, if that's the difficulty ... ' said Miss Hoare. At the bar of the Saracen's Head she loomed brazenly above a knot of Summer People in khaki shorts and sunhats and announced: 'Two glasses of white wine. And this young man is my nephew.' Later, as they sat in an alcove looking out over the humped keels of upended crab boats, she said: 'Will it matter? Saying you're my nephew, I mean.' 'I shouldn't think my father will be very pleased.' 'Will he find out?' 'Oh, I expect someone will tell him,' Julian told her, elated by

the wine and not caring very much. 'They usually do.'

August came, with flaring skies. An old man had a heart attack on the beach, and an air-sea rescue helicopter came to ferry him away. The O level results were due in a week. 'Exams,' Miss Hoare pronounced, 'are the curse of the educated classes.' They were in the Saracen's Head again, whose staff, curiously, had yet to complain to Mr Holroyd. 'Are you still set on Art?' She enunciated it as one would the name of a favourite relative or a honeymoon destination. 'I don't know,' Julian wondered, realising that for all his disparagement of mathematics, physics, chemistry and the dreary people who taught them, he really did not know. 'There's an art school at Norwich, 'he explained. 'Or even at Lowestoft. And then ... ' Miss Hoare beamed back at him. Reckoning up the number of glasses of white wine she had consumed, Julian calculated it at six or perhaps seven. 'You must lend me those sketchbooks of yours,' she said. 'Let me look at them and see what can be done. It may take a day or so because I've got a friend arriving, but then I'll have a look and we'll see what can be done.' And Julian, glimpsing his face suddenly in the glass of the window, felt the kind of wild excitement he had once experienced as a child watching the Lancaster bombers veer inland from the sea towards the RAF stations of the Norfolk plain.

Mr Castleton, Miss Hoare's friend, was a thin, red-haired man in an outsize

purple blazer and a cravat, who made himself unpopular in the town within half an hour of his arrival by parking his car across a narrow street entrance and then remonstrating with the people who tried to remove it. Subsequently he antagonised Mr Holroyd by asking for a copy of *Health and Efficiency*. 'I told him,' Mr Holroyd reported testily, 'that if he wanted pornography he could go to Cromer for it.' He and Miss Hoare dined noisily at the Saracen's Head and were seen picnicking on the cliff. Once, passing them in the crowded market square, Julian was certain that they saw him, but the wave went unacknowledged. No word came about the sketchbooks.

The O level results arrived on a grey Saturday morning. Julian felt his hand tremble a little as he turned over the brown, rectangular envelope he remembered addressing to himself six weeks before. He need not have worried. 'An excellent set of results,' Mr Holroyd crowed. 'And especially in Science. I must confess I'm gratified.' With some ceremony he presented Julian with a creased ten shilling note. Knocking at the door of Miss Hoare's cottage an hour later, Julian realised that he had still made no decision, that the tangle of contending paths still ran away before him. Some time later the door was opened, with bad grace, by Mr Castleton. He wore a pair of ancient, buttonless pajamas and was smoking a cigarette. Mr Castleton examined Julian without interest. 'It's your artist friend,' he said over his shoulder. Back in the belly of the house came the noise of a vague, indeterminate movement. 'She's sozzled,' Mr Castleton said ruthlessly. 'Pissed. You understand what I mean? One over the eight. Here. Better take these while you' re here.' Stooping to retrieve the sketchbooks in their brown wrapping, Julian saw, a room away, the lurching figure: nightdress awry, wild, staring face, one eye blinking in confusion. 'Go on, piss off,' Mr Castleton said equably.

Towards lunchtime, as the wind whipped up, he stood on the low, rocky promontory overlooking the station, where Summer People with bags and suitcases laboured towards the waiting train. Then, with one of those sharp, decisive gestures that define our lives, he began to tear up the books, one by one, casting each fragment out onto the swelling breeze. Later the rain came in, noisily, across the long bar of the sea. ◗

PETER SOMMER TRAVELS

"A perfect combination of intellectual, aesthetic, sensual and physical experiences."

EXPERT-LED ARCHAEOLOGICAL & CULTURAL TOURS FOR SMALL GROUPS

ONE OF THE WORLD'S "TOP TEN LEARNING RETREATS"
- NATIONAL GEOGRAPHIC

WALKING AND CRUISING THE CARIAN COAST

WALKING AND CRUISING THE LYCIAN SHORE

WALKING AND CRUISING WESTERN LYCIA

EXPLORING CRETE

EXPLORING SICILY

EXPLORING THE PELOPONNESE

A GASTRONOMIC CRUISE IN TURKEY

CRUISING TO THE CYCLADES

CRUISING DALMATIA FROM ŠIBENIK TO ZADAR

Don't call me luvvie...

...or smirk knowingly and say 'resting' when I'm actually unemployed. *Jonathan Cecil* on phrases and stereotypes guaranteed to send an actor into a rage

One of my least favourite and, alas, all too frequent real-life scenarios goes like this:
Fellow Party-Guest: *What do you do?*
Myself: *I'm an actor.*
FPG: *Really - what are you in?*
Myself: *Nothing at present.*
FPG: *Ah (with a sort of amused and knowing triumph) RESTING!*

At which point I edge away – concealing, I hope successfully, pique and, above all, embarrassment.

I feel embarrassed for the FPGs. They think that they are using the correct 'in' jargon, whereas in over 30 years as an actor I have never heard a fellow-professional use the term 'resting' to mean out of work.

The expression, if it was ever used, belongs to the era of the old Victorian ham beloved of Punch cartoons – lank-haired and red-nosed, in an astrakhan collar and a sombrero, he greets a colleague with 'What news on the Rialto, laddie?' before touching him for a half-sovereign.

To speak of actors 'resting' today is like saying to a modern schoolboy, 'I bet you get up to some spiffing japes in the tuck shop.' It also implies that such idleness is not enforced but a matter of carefree choice. The idea of an unemployed actor appears as much a matter for clichéd hilarity as a stingy Scotsman or a henpecked husband – though no one rocks with mirth at the thought of a redundant bank manager or a briefless barrister. Many people, it seems, regard actors – working or not – as intrinsically ridiculous.

This conclusion is reinforced by a new horror: the current expression 'luvvie'. It has the same contemptuous resonance as 'resting', and is almost as absurdly out of date. I have heard theatre people calling

each other 'lovey', but not many and certainly not recently. As used in *Private Eye* and the tabloids, 'luvvie' suggests a successful, fashionable show-person, but I connect it with the seedier repertory players of my youth – usually in sarcastic mood: 'Don't you know your lines, luvvie?' Terms like 'Darling' and 'Sweetheart' are still fairly common in the theatre – often as handy substitutes for momentarily forgotten names.

As a newcomer I found such gushing endearments, however insincere, a liberating change from public-school reserve. It was delightfully incongruous to hear a non-effeminate hulk like Robert Morley call Gielgud 'John darling'.

These days theatricality is decidedly unfashionable, and 'luvvie', with its breathless, stagestruck overtones, seems peculiarly inept when applied to the modem, laid-back generation. Nowadays for one young player to say of another, 'He, or she, is not a typical actor' is invariably complimentary, though

I'm increasingly unsure of what a typical actor actually is.

In my early days, there were certain definite stereotypes - sometimes tiresome, always amusing to observe.

The Shakespeareans, flamboyantly resonant in pubs ('Another pint if you will, dearest heart!') and dressed with somewhat studied untidiness, were in sharp contrast with the immaculately suited variety types, competitively swapping gags ('Working well tonight!' if the gag got a laugh, 'Went down better first house!' if it didn't).

The late 1950s brought in a new breed of working-class actor – determinedly anti-actorish, but with their own kind of Brando-inspired moodiness. These were counterbalanced by the raffish, self-consciously posh set, epitomised by the recently departed Ronnie Fraser, whose lives seemed to revolve round bars and quitting rehearsals on the dot of one o'clock, ('This is the time of day when I generally repair to the nearest local hostelry...')

Conversation among most pros appeared to be dominated by anecdotes, divisible into the good, the bad and the trad. The good ones depended largely on the teller, and were vivid, original and personal. The bad had seemingly no point at all except that they featured a famous name, enabling the raconteur – usually male – to demonstrate a) his gift for mimicry and b) his intimate acquaintance with the great ('old Johnny G' or 'Darling Dame Peg, bless her'). Trad anecdotes could be good or bad, but had been handed down and embellished by generations of thespians and were shamelessly attributed to all manner of different protagonists, depending on whose voices were most easily imitable: Ralph Richardson, John Gielgud and Edith Evans being particular favourites, even if the stories didn't quite fit them.

It is partly because of such dated thespian stereotypes that actors are still considered ridiculous. But jealousy comes into it as well: it is hard to match actors – vain and childish as they can be – for perennially young enthusiasm, warm camaraderie and sheer high spirits. Perhaps we should be less sensitive and more defiantly bohemian; proud to be outsiders.

About to embark on my stage career I was asked by an appalled upper-class hostess: 'Won't you meet the most frightful people?'

'No more than in other professions' was my youthful reply: a trifle pompous but still, I think, correct. Yet now and again I wish I had answered simply:

'I hope so.' ◑

VIDEO
LARRY ADLER

On the Town 1949, £10.99
It took the considerable talents of Gene Kelly, Frank Sinatra, Betty Garrett and Ann Miller to make this witless, pathetic film. These people are stars and, according to Frank Capra's book title, a star means, 'Name above the title'. Yet the only medal worth awarding is to Jules Munshin, whose name is below the title. Mr Munshin is as genuinely funny as Kelly and Sinatra are not, and is, to this jaundiced observer, the one person worth watching.

The music follows the pattern of A L Webber, one tune running relentlessly through the picture (though Webber may not have been born when this epic was made). The tune is *New York, New York*, and in this instance to play it even once seems too much. Gene Kelly is director as well as actor. (He shares the direction with Stanley Donen so the dancing crimes must be attributable to him.) Everything is at the tempo of manic hysteria. No one walks when they can run, most dialogue is yelled rather than spoken. I can't remember a single relaxed moment in the film. There is one glorious gag. A superbly ugly girl sneezes, Kelly says, 'Gesundheit!' and the girl, looking at him adoringly, says, 'That's the nicest thing anyone ever said to me.'

Unfortunately Kelly has to dumb down (see how quickly I absorb the jargon) his dancing when he has routines with Sinatra and Munshin, which is most of the time, and always to that irritating tune. The only way Ann Miller is distinguishable from her co-star Vera-Ellen is that Miss Miller is brunette while Miss Vera-Ellen is blonde. Betty Garrett is good and funny when she's given a chance, which isn't often enough.

How can such a shallow script have come from Betty Comden and Adolph Green? I first saw them in a night-club act, *The Revuers*. Another member was Judith Tuvim who, when she went into the movies, became Judy Holliday. The routine that Kelly performs, while Sinatra and Munshin tag along, could have come from a high-school production.

A tip: try to miss the last 15 minutes or so. Then you won't have to look at that pompous and needlessly complicated ballet.

The Thirty-Nine Steps 1935, £6.99
The makers off *On the Town* could profitably have studied this film before lurching into their own phoney frenzy. Here is a picture with real pace. It moves like Schumacher on the racetrack, yet everything seems right and natural, nothing is contrived. Robert Donat moves effortlessly, delivering excitement, even terror, without strain. It is simply a faultless film, superbly cast with Madeleine Carroll, Godfrey Tearle, Lucie Mannheim and Peggy Ashcroft, and directed by... who else?... Alfred Hitchcock.

In my memory, there are two vivid moments. One is when Godfrey Tearle, as the suave villain, holds up his hand to reveal a missing finger joint, thus telling Donat that he is the murderer. (The other is Charles Laughton in his classic role as Henry VIII, about to enter the bedroom of the detested Catherine of Aragon. He looks straight into camera and says, as only Laughton could, 'The things I've done for England!')

You know with an Adler review there is a certain amount of name-dropping. (My brother wanted me to call my autobiography, 'Name Drops Keep Falling on My Head'.) Thus I will mention that Ingrid Bergman told me that the worst thing about working with Hitchcock was his habit of visiting her in her dressing-room and trying to make a pass.

If you think I'm the lousiest of film reviewers, as one writer to the last issue does, get *The Thirty-Nine Steps*, after which you'll nominate me as one of the best in the business.

Barry Cryer finally gets a word in about his fellow
Old Fart and comic genius Willie Rushton

That was Willie, that was

I can't remember where and when I first met Willie and neither could he. In the same way, I can't remember where and when I first met Racquel Welch, but that may be due to the fact that I never did. Willie always maintained that we must have met 'somewhere round the back of David Frost', and that was probably true.

Willie, was, of course, a founder member of *That Was the Week That Was*, not to mention *Private Eye* (so I won't). My wife and I went to witness the pilot programme of *TW3*. It ran some two and three-quarter hours, as I remember. Millicent Martin was going on holiday as soon as she'd sung her opening song and the folk tale had it that she was in Spain before the programme finished.

But back to Willie. We didn't meet that night, but I do remember enjoying this fleshy-faced, beardless youth, with his droll voice and an uncanny ability to become Harold Macmillan. It's surprising to recall the impact that had in those days – someone actually impersonating the Prime Minister. Peter Cook had already done his own hilarious demolition job on stage in *Beyond the Fringe*, but I think Willie was the first on television.

We finally worked together on a programme rather snappily titled *The New Stars and Garters*, an updated version of a pub-based show I had already worked on. Willie and his wife Dorgan were featured, but it didn't set the ratings on fire.

We became friends, but didn't work together on a regular basis until the birth of *I'm Sorry I Haven't a Clue* on Radio 4 in 1972. Tim Brooke-Taylor, Graeme

Garden and I were already on board, with chairman Humphrey Lyttelton, but after the departure of John Cleese, Bill Oddie and Jo Kendall, who didn't enjoy the ad lib free-for-all of it, Willie was invited to join, by common consent.

Talking of common consent, Willie would invariably go against any consensus of opinion. Once a decision, apparently acceptable to all, had been reached at any meeting, he would suddenly discover a reason why it should not be acted upon. This was more out of his innate sense of mischief than anything else, but it led to some spirited exchanges. When he died, I had this fantasy that someone said to him: 'I hear you died in December, Willie.' 'No, not me – where did you hear that?'

In 1990, we were invited by the Spinal Injuries Association to do an evening in the theatre. We asked Graeme, an anarchic stand-up/juggler, Pierre Hollins, and the singer Christine Pilgrim to join us, with the stalwart Colin Sell at the piano. We did this for the first time at the City Varieties music hall in my home town of Leeds. Willie drew the raffle at the interval, with merry cries of 'Pink 32!', and I still remember a good burgher arriving on the stage to collect his prize – a small man of forbidding aspect. He didn't utter a word. 'Have you a smile about your person?' carolled Willie, and the man took his envelope and departed. Willie beamed at the audience. 'And now for the next miserable Yorkshire bastard,' he boomed.

We then did dates round the country and in 1991 Willie said to me, 'Let's see if there's any money in this.' His son, Toby, was about to present a student production of *The Duchess of Malfi*, or 'What's it all about, Malfi?', as Willlie dubbed it, on the Edinburgh Fringe. He rang up the owner of the venue and asked if he would like a late-night show to follow the play. The reply was in the affirmative, so we journeyed up, bearing posters drawn by Willie. I still think his incredible talent as an artist, not just a cartoonist, has not been acknowledged. We arrived to be greeted by the news that we were sold out for the week. And so *Two Old Farts in the Night* was bom. The title was Willie's idea – he said we couldn't be done under the Trades Descriptions Act. We subsequently toured until his death in 1996.

What can I say about him, that he wouldn't interrupt? One story: He sat one night at the top table at a dinner. The chairman of the company, who I shall call Sir Charles – for that was his name – was talking loudly into Willie's left ear as he ate, with Willie murmuring, 'Good Lord,' and, I can imagine,' at suitable intervals. Finally the man said, in front of the whole table, 'You'd better be funny tonight Mr Rushton, we're paying you a lot of money.' 'Well, most of it's for sitting with you,' responded Willie.

His ashes are buried by the boundary at the Oval. This has denied him the pleasure of the inscription he wanted on his gravestone. He saw the word 'Discontinued': 'That's what I want!' Discontinued? Him? Never. Cheers, Will. ◑

Opposite page, top: Richard Ingrams and Willie Rushton at work in the *Private Eye* offices. Bottom: The Two Old Farts. This page, top: cover of the first birthday edition of *The Oldie*, showing (clockwise) Naim Attallah, Barry Humphries, Germaine Greer, Richard Ingrams and Auberon Waugh. Left: The origins of the *Oldie* symbol. Below: 'Grey Power' oldie man

'Have you a smile about your person? carolled Willie'

Interview

Brian Sewell

Naim Attallah in conversation with the *Evening Standard*'s outspoken art critic

You are a distinguished art historian, but it is as art critic that you have earned yourself a reputation – indeed you might easily be called the doyen of art criticism. Is it one from which you derive satisfaction?

Oh dear, I think I have to argue with several of those statements. I have absolutely no distinction as an art historian. I've never written the book I want to write, and I've never been involved in a major exhibition, at least not since I was a mere boy. When I first left the Courtauld I had a very promising career. I was regarded as quite a bright boy and it all looked as though it was set fair. Then I was offered a job at Christie's and I spent the next ten years of my life there being diverted from serious scholarship. Working at Christie's is a game of swift judgement and even swifter identification, or sometimes mis-identification. I became a critic by accident. I had spent my whole life up to that point looking at pictures, going to exhibitions and experiencing the frisson of excitement as things changed in the contemporary art world. As a student of art history, I was very much aware of what David Hockney and his contemporaries tried to do, and I had considerable sympathy with them. But I now find myself very detached from those revolutionaries of the Sixties and Seventies, having grown old with them, as it were. I have come to realise how trivial and idiotic much of post-war art is.

Flaubert said: 'A man is a critic when he cannot be an artist, in the same way that a man becomes an informer when he cannot be a soldier.' Do you think there is an uncomfortable truth in that view?

No. I don't think there is any truth in that at all. Edward Lucie-Smith, for example, did not become a critic because he couldn't paint. Edward came to criticism from poetry, from being a writer, from an interest in acquiring things, which led him naturally to the intellectual pursuit

of what lies behind the things we acquire; it has absolutely nothing to do with his inability to draw or paint.

Oscar Wilde had a different perspective from Flaubert, believing that it is precisely because a man cannot do a thing that he is the proper judge of it. Are you any more inclined to the Wildean view of things?

I'm not, but the last Conservative Government was, and this new Labour regime quite certainly is. There is a belief among those who have the power to make important appointments that the amateur is best. This applies particularly in the area of visual arts. It is the devil of the art gallery and the museum in this country that their trustees are amateurs, and it is the devil of organisations like the Museums and Galleries Commission that their commissioners are people who know absolutely nothing about the history and purpose of galleries and museums. So don't blame the critic; blame the Government.

Your father committed suicide before you were born, and your mother by all

accounts was stiflingly possessive. How does a child survive such a childhood?

I think I survived my childhood because my mother treated me from my very earliest consciousness as an adult. The consequence was that when I eventually went to school, very soon after my 11th birthday, my abilities were absurd for a child of my age. I had a considerable command of things like Greek mythology, Roman history and opera, and I read the novels that my mother read instead of baby books. This was rather unbalanced in one way, but it gave me a head start in terms of general culture. I was taken to the National Gallery every week as a child. I don't know what I would have done had my mother not brought me up in such a one-sided way, but her one side opened windows all the time. That is why I didn't stifle.

You have said of your father's suicide that he put the cat out before he gassed himself. How important was it for you to be made aware of that gentle and humane touch before an act of such self-destructiveness?

Insofar as I have any folk memory, as it were, of my father, it is the thing that means most to me. I share my father's melancholy nature and there are moments when depression becomes unbearable, but what prevents me from committing suicide is that I have dogs. And I care more for them than I do for myself.

There was presumably a temptation to romanticise the father you had never known...

No. In the very early days his absence was really not important. My life was very full with the entertainments provided by my mother. And by the age of 11 I had acquired a stepfather who was interested in music and religion, and also in the observances of the Church of England, as opposed to the Roman Catholic Church in which I had been christened. So there were plenty of things to excite and divert me from worrying or wondering about my own father.

Did you consciously decide against having children of your own, and if so, was this related to your own experience as a child?

I went through a period in my early thirties when I thought that it would be wonderful if one could settle down and lead the absolutely conventional life, marriage and children, and so on. But I knew deep down that this was an impossibility – I had been solitary for so long. I also had to confront the irredeemable nature of my homosexuality, which at an early stage had come into extreme conflict with my religious life. This wasn't exactly straightforward because I had been born a Roman Catholic, and though I had been diverted into the Church of England by my stepfather, I had always wanted to go back to being a Roman. But what disturbed me was the hostility of both branches of the Christian Church to what was my essential nature. Like all men I am a sexual being; it need not be very fruitfully applied, but it cannot be denied.

You turned down a place at Oxford in favour of the Courtauld Institute. You have said that your time at the Courtauld taught you how to look properly at a picture. Do you think this is something which has to be learned?

One can look at pictures in so many different ways. You can look at a picture like a clerk: how big is it, what is it made of, what is the medium, to whom did it belong, where has it been, who has written about it? And you accumulate all that information and you never ask yourself whether it is good or great or whether it excites you; it is simply documented. There are an awful lot of art historians like that. And then there are other people who just look at a picture and say, isn't it wonderful? They are sent witless in front of abstracts by Mark Rothko, trying to induce some trance-like state as a result of sitting in front of a sea of colour. That's also pretty uninformed. One definitely needs a bit more than that. For myself, I need to respond not only to the dry documentation of a picture; I want to respond to the working of the painter's hand and brush, I want to see the lifting-off point, that little tail of paint when you take a brush away, I

Mantegna's Christ: 'the face is full of pain... you sense that after being three days dead the blood is flowing again'

want to see when something is in pastel, when something is in glaze, I want to involve myself in the act of painting in exactly the same way as when playing a musical instrument one is somehow involved in the mind of the composer. There's a wonderful little picture by Mantegna which is always called *The Entombment of Christ*, but I think it's the Resurrection, because the usual paraphernalia of the entombment are not there. Christ is being propped up on the narrow end of a sarcophagus by two angels, both of whom have one leg in the sarcophagus, and they seem to me to be heaving him out of it rather than laying him in it. His lower limbs are over the edge to the fore of the picture and the face is full of pain; it's the most agonised face you could hope to find in the whole history of art. The body is pallid and the face is ruddy, and you sense that after being three days dead the blood is flowing again – think of the excruciating pain that you experience when you've been sleeping on your arm, and the blood begins to flood into it again. This is what Christ is experiencing over his whole body. If you can look at a picture like this and see those things, then I think you are seeing everything that you can.

How does this fit with your view that good art should be accessible to all and that there is something in a Donatello or a Michelangelo that can be understood by every man?

I cannot imagine that even the humblest Florentine peasant on seeing Donatello's *Habakkuk* would not immediately recognise it for what it was. Similarly, a French peasant coming into contact with Rodin's *Burghers of Calais* would immediately understand, perhaps not the historical story, but from the expressions, from the body language of those figures, they would know exactly what was happening – all the information is there. But you look at contemporary art now, what is to be divined from 99 per cent of it? Absolutely nothing. And when lecturers in galleries like the Tate are asked, 'What does this picture mean?' the answer is invariably, 'Oh, it means what you want it to mean.' This just isn't good enough.

You deplore the breed of artist who urinates in the snow and makes bronze casts of the result, and there are many people who agree with you. Do you believe that there are objective standards by which we can judge what we might call real works of art as opposed to fashionable, gimmicky pieces?

The short answer to that is no, because if you apply objective standards you will get no advance. You might condemn new ways of doing things, as 19th-century academic painters condemned the Impressionists. Having said that, I do have very serious problems with so-called artists like Helen Chadwick, because it seems to me that neither her *Piss Flowers*, as these snow pieces were called, nor her *Chocolate Fountain*, which was a pure reference to the emptying of the bowels, could possibly constitute works of art. If they are works of performance, then perhaps their place is in the theatre, but not in the art gallery.

One of the central difficulties for anyone who is interested in art is what might be called the matter of taste. Is it possible to say, for example, that David Hockney is not to my liking, not my taste, but I recognise that he is an important artist?

I could demonstrate to anyone who would care to listen to me that David Hockney is a rotten painter. In the late Sixties and the first half of

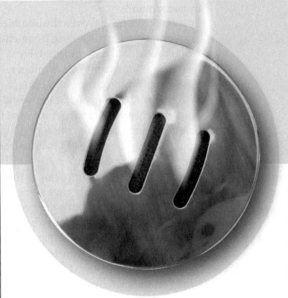

the Seventies he became, fairly briefly, a brilliant draughtsman. David is somebody who does not understand the paint; he has absolutely no feeling for it other than as colour between lines, absolutely none. He talks a great deal about perspective, but he has no sense of aerial perspective, nor does he know anything about varying colour, nothing at all.

To what, then, do you attribute his rise to fame?
Entirely to his homosexuality. He came in as a flamboyant homosexual at just the right moment in the Sixties when everyone for the first time ever was determined to be liberal about it. People who were not themselves homosexual would buy David's work and hang it in the drawing-room as a demonstration of their own liberal attitudes, and it's just gone on from there. Once you entrench a painter in the public mind as the great painter of the day, he goes on as such. We are now turning him into a guru.

One problem, I suppose, is that we know that when people saw the pictures of Manet or Cézanne over a century ago, they seemed outrageously modern and people and felt that everything that they had known and loved about art hitherto was under threat. Are we bad at dealing with the shock of the new?
No. You just have to consider the history of collecting to dispute that. I mean, Degas had an agent in Manchester, for God's sake. That doesn't suggest to me that there was no appreciation. Or if you look at the great Scottish collections, there were some farsighted Scottish dealers selling wonderful pictures to people who built ships. Then there's that old foolishness about all the Impressionists dying in poverty. They didn't. It cost Monet just ten pictures to buy Giverny, that's all. He was turning out a picture a day, and he was a rich man. Degas was rich, and Renoir was also rich. Gauguin and Van Gogh were the odd men out; you can't apply their level of penury to all the others. I simply do not understand how this myth survives. Of course, there have always been opponents, but right across Europe there have been collectors and dealers who have supported the painters at the time – you only have to look at how early their work was being bought by major institutions. In the Neue Pinakothek in Munich there is a wonderful picture by Manet, a kind of breakfast picture – I can't remember what it is called. It didn't have to hang around a studio. There were great German dealers in places like Düsseldorf – Düsseldorf, for heaven's sake, the Manchester of Germany!

Conceptual art leaves you cold – there is nothing, you say, that lifts the spirit. Can you be sure, however, that there is nothing that lifts the spirit of others?
That isn't quite my view. Let's take something which is possibly a familiar example: the first set of cage pieces by Damien Hirst. These are glass containers with steel frames and when they were exhibited in the ICA some years ago I was deeply moved by them. They were very disturbing. They were not beautiful, but they did what beauty does, which is affect the spirit. Which is why I am very defensive of Damien, because he has gone through phases which are not just flamboyant things with sharks and sheep; he has also touched on things that are essential to the darker side of human nature. My esteem for his work is very high.

A few years ago you said: 'It is terribly disturbing to find oneself literally loathed by people. I hardly go out at all now, except to go to galleries.' Has that situation changed at all, or are you still disturbed by the strength of people's reactions to you?
I am disturbed, yes. I have become something of a recluse, and I now very largely no longer go to the press views of exhibitions in case those who most dislike me are there. My presence seems to disturb them even more than their reaction disturbs me. There was one woman critic, for example, who had a fit of hysterics at the Royal Academy and said she couldn't bear to be in the same room. She just screamed to the company at large, 'There's that terrible man!' She tried to go to another room but found she couldn't get out because she was at the end of the sequence of rooms. So I just said, 'Oh, sod the bloody woman. I'll leave and come back when she gets herself out of the gallery.' And I left.

But by holding such strong views don't you invite strong reactions? Your writing style is provocative, and some would also argue that it is gratuitously insulting and also sometimes designed to hurt. If you feel wounded and distressed by people's loathing of you, aren't you also engaged in dishing out hatred and venom to others, who presumably feel pain and distress just as you do?
I only ever write about people and exhibitions which are there as targets. I am in awe of no institution, so if an exhibition is put on at the Royal Academy or the National Gallery and it seems to me to be shoddily done, then I will say so. If there is an exhibition of, let's say, the early works of Gainsborough at the National Gallery, and they are so foolish that they can't see they've got the order wrong or they have simply not understood the material, then they deserve to be slaughtered for it, because they of all people should know how to do it. I very rarely tackle a young painter. I will tackle an old one who is well established, like Lucian Freud or John Wonnacott, a British representational artist. I would normally never think about writing about him, except that he is suddenly thrust under my nose as one of the great figurative painters of the late 20th century. Well, he is nothing of the kind. I feel challenged, so I respond. But at the same time I write quite a lot of letters to painters who are virtually unknown. I am invited to their exhibitions, and if I go then I think they deserve some comment. That way they are not exposed in the *Evening Standard*, no damage is done, and I haven't been beastly to them in public, which is what I am always accused of.

But do you ever worry about the effect that your attack might have on the person who is under attack?
I think it's fair game. If a man has put himself forward, or is put forward

by his dealer for gain, then he must take what comes. It's absurd that he should ask for praise and then be angry if he gets something other than praise. One of the most disagreeable things that ever happened to me was going to an exhibition and bumping into Lawrence Gowing, who at one point had been my tutor. He put his arm round me and told me that he hoped I would give the painter unalloyed praise. If you knew how much Lawrence spat when he said the consonant P, you would have some idea of how unpleasant this was. But the real unpleasantness lay in his expectation of unalloyed praise for a boy who was a pupil of his, just because he was his pupil and because Gowing thought he ought to be pushed. This is not good enough. Art is much more important than the people who make it.

In your article on Clause 28 in the *Evening Standard* you wrote that a man's sexuality is deeply determined, and that we all know what we are well before the onset of puberty. What do you think about the concerns of Baroness Young that standards of decency and morality are at risk if Clause 28 is repealed?
I don't think that any boy – I can't speak for girls, I know so little about them – is ever diverted from his sexual path by the alternative. He always knows what it is. About 20 years after I left school one of the few boys I had kept in touch with decided to give a dinner party for our contemporaries. There were about 40 people there, men and their wives, with me the only unmarried one there. The wives seemed to me to be largely vain and silly women who were talking boastfully about their aspirations for their children and so on. At some point homosexuality came into the general discussion and during one of those crystal moments when nobody is talking, I suddenly heard myself say, 'I think I've had enough of this debate. There isn't a single man here with whom I have not had sex. And on that note I shall bid you all farewell.' The point of that story is that I had had sex with every one of those boys, and they had all married and had children. I was the queer one. They were all normal. So whatever we did together – and they were perfectly happy to have sex with me – our sexual drives were established well before we were involved in any way with each other. I am convinced that we are what we are at a very early stage.

In the same article, you refer to the 'righteous' Cardinal Winning and his 'hysterical bigotry'. Cardinal Winning is deeply conservative on issues such as homosexuality and abortion. When it comes to art, many people would argue that you too are deeply conservative. What distinguishes your own approach from that of Cardinal Winning?
[Laughs] I think you are too clever by half. But it's actually quite an easy question to answer in the sense that in the art world there hasn't been enough time for the dross to fall away. With the passage of time, people will begin to sort the wheat from the chaff. The advantage of being a critic is that one can begin that sorting process very much earlier than an institution like the Tate can. The art world would benefit from the odd bit of discipline, somebody to say, 'This is not art – whatever it is, it isn't art.' But going back to your basic point, to me being the Cardinal Winning of the art world, I don't think that's true. There are things that excite me, there are things which from time to time get through what may seem to be my carapace of prejudice.

What place does love have in your life? Do you fall in love easily?
I have been deeply in love with the same man for almost 30 years. He's married, he's on his second marriage, in fact, but the love isn't quite unrequited. Occasionally I leave a message on my answering machine which says, 'I am busy committing adultery. Please leave your number and I will return your call when I stop for coffee.' And it's true, because although I am not married in any sense other than to him, he is committing adultery, so I share it.

Your love of animals is well known. Do you feel they are safer than people, perhaps, more loyal, more lovable?
The care I give to a bird with a broken wing is not conditional on being

rewarded with loyalty and love. But the wonderful thing about owning dogs, and to a lesser extent cats, is that you do get a response which is human in some degree, or recognisably of the same nature as a human response, but that's a bonus. If I had the opportunity to live my life again knowing what I know now, I would not be an art historian, I would be a vet.

Would you say, perhaps, that it is almost as difficult not to believe as to believe?
I think it depends entirely on your background. If I had had no background in the Church, then I don't think I would have any longing to join it. It would be enormously comforting to be able to return to a belief, but I don't think I shall. My lack of faith is supported everywhere I look – Rwanda, Kosovo, Bosnia. Where is God?

Your stand against religion seemed to waver when you had your heart attack and then a heart bypass operation. Indeed you told the staff that if anything went wrong they were to send for a priest. Was this a version of Pascal's wager?
[Laughs] No, it was an entirely unconscious reaction. The nursing sister had challenged me with her brisk, bright, businesslike approach, and with her clipboard in hand she told me there were one or two details which had to be settled, one being that I was down as an atheist. Although one feels more dead than alive in such a situation, I said, 'No, no, I'm not an atheist. I am an agnostic, but if anything goes wrong, call a priest.' It was purely instinctive. Besides, I see absolutely nothing wrong with going through the motions of the Roman Catholic preparations for death, which can be very beautiful and moving.

Are you resigned to oblivion when you die, or would you like to think that there might be an afterlife?
Of course I'm resigned to oblivion. The great book on Michelangelo is not written. It won't be on anybody's shelf. That is the only afterlife I should have liked, to have written that book, and I now know I shan't. I suspect I shall die in harness with the *Evening Standard*, scribbling ephemera. And the book won't be there. 🔵

Brian Sewell: 15th July 1931- 19th September 2015

'Does it contain nuts?'

Sound & Fury

Save our radio!

Blow the telly – scrapping the licence fee would seriously threaten our treasured 80-year-old tradition of public service wireless broadcasting, says *Libby Purves*

There is a vigorous campaign going on to get rid of the licence fee. It could, I suppose, work. Anything can happen. The idea that 'human rights' are compromised by having to buy a TV licence before you can see any news at all is on the face of it quite winning: think how dreadful it would be if you weren't allowed to buy The *Oldie* without paying to support the *Spectator* and the *Radio Times* as well. As for the counter-argument that the BBC provides a unique public service, that has its problems too: in a world where TV channels breed like earwigs and all of them scramble for ratings, it is harder and harder to maintain that there are certain types of programme that only the BBC will or could do. Myself, I think it's worth it, just about, to have some telly at least uninterrupted by crass advertisements for greasy crisps and equally greasy compensation lawyers, but an increasingly vociferous lobby is furious that even if you never watch a single pixel of BBC TV, you can't own a telly without paying £112 a year.

You can see their logic: yet the argument leaves out one vital thing that nobody ever seems to mention. Public service broadcasting, founded and so eccentrically funded 80 years ago, is not just about television. The BBC, its charter, and its quaint licence fee arrangement were founded long before Logie Baird got round to sending pictures. The BBC was born as a radio broadcaster, and radio still lies at its heart, holding its soul and conscience. The separate radio licence withered away decades back; it is the so-called TV licence fee which funds Radios 1 to 5, local radio and the new digital networks.

It is radio's meagre but significant

ILLUSTRATION BY PHILIP THOMPSON

Oh, how we love the 1948 programme guidelines banning all mention of lodgers, underwear or baskets

share of the licence fee that pays Jenni Murray and Sara Cox, Peter Donaldson and Charlotte Green; the satirists of *The News Quiz* and the anarchs of *I'm Sorry I Haven't a Clue*. It pays for *Law in Action*, *Start the Week*, *File on Four*, *Choral Evensong*, *Night Waves*, *Desert Island Discs*. It funds producers, researchers, operators of free helplines on everything from consumer law to education, programme websites enabling you to hear a show again, hours of wonderful drama, the rather less wonderful *Archers*, all manner of intriguing and affable waffle on programmes like mine, and a slew of local radio stations. It is, if you will excuse an un-BBC like expression, bloody good value.

I have been considering the history and nature of radio for a book: part memoir, part celebration, part history*. What became ever clearer to me is that the richness of UK radio is entirely due to the way it was set up. A cadre of idealists under John Reith was set free to invent a use for the magical new technology; and although their caution and prudery was sometimes ludicrous (oh, how we love the 1948 programme guidelines banning all mention of lodgers, underwear or baskets!) their mission was essentially a noble one.

They seriously wanted to bring the best of culture, music, thought and public affairs to everyone: Reith spoke of 'a return to the city state of old' and his deputy captain, C A Lewis, spoke of the aerials in the street as 'spears against the sky' in the fight against ignorance and loneliness. These chaps were into social inclusion 70 years before the phrase was coined. They wanted to share.

Radio is a tremendous medium: simple, cheap, evocative and stirring, nimble, fast-reacting and unpretentious. Because its speakers must make sense without the help of pretty shrugs and pouts, what it says is more sharply remembered than much TV. It is a grand antidote to the celebrity culture, because whereas a celeb on television is something interesting to gawp at, if he or she is talking rubbish it is the radio listener who notices first.

Because it is a cheap medium, based on thought rather than pictures, it often gets the stories early: *Food Programme* listeners knew about BSE long before anyone else. And radio suits busy, active, responsible lives.

I know people who left school early – at 14, the older ones – and for whom

Radio 4 has been their university and their friend. Poor or busy, carers and parents, craftsmen or delivery drivers, they have used it to keep in the swim, up to speed, in touch with the culture; to share national moments and national jokes. Not everyone listens to Radios 4 and 5 – some prefer a diet of music. But if you want all these riches they are there for you, free and uncompromised by government interference. It is a democratic marvel.

But its strengths are the reason why it is hard to fund good radio through advertising. Watching TV you are sitting down, part of a big passive audience. Listening to the radio you are an active individual, getting on with your day. So you get far more irritated by someone talking meretricious garbage on the radio than you do on TV; on the other hand, because they are speaking in real time

If you want all these riches they are there for you, free and uncompromised. It is a democratic marvel

you can't skip, as you do with print. Adding advertisements to radio hugely degrades the experience.

There are good commercial stations, among them now a quality speech station, Oneword; but nobody can deny that the adverts are a terrible intrusion, far worse than on TV.

So, what would happen if the licence went? Would BBC radio be thrown to the commercial wolves? We'd hate that. A pure radio licence would be unpoliceable: easy enough when a radio was a big brown thing with valves, but impossible now with radios the size of a button, or built into clocks, or coming through the Internet.

Direct government funding would fatally compromise radio's ability to challenge politicians. So how would you keep this treasure safe, with no licence fee? The trouble is that while you can – just about – make the case that BBC television does nothing that commercial TV doesn't duplicate, BBC radio is unique. And, speaking strictly as a listener, I think it's really rather wonderful. What would you do?

WH Auden

WH AUDEN came to stay at our house in Birmingham in summer 1967. My father, Richard Hoggart, had proposed him for an honorary degree, and offered to put him up. Auden had been raised in Birmingham and said he was happy to see the place again. In fact, he spent a large part of his time in a deckchair in the garden, chain-smoking Lucky Strikes.

I had read little of his work, and was afraid of being grilled about it. In fact he didn't want to talk about poetry much at all; instead his mealtime conversation was more mundane. One dinner time he devoted in part to persuading my mother that she should buy a Kenwood food mixer because it was much better than rival mixers. What did command attention was that famous face, just as astounding a topographical marvel of ravines, canyons and dry gullies as the photographs showed. And his voice was a strange mixture of English and American, with an admixture of German, since he lived half the year in Austria.

On the evening Auden arrived, my parents had invited friends and colleagues round to meet him. I was put in charge of drinks. Auden bustled into the kitchen and asked if I knew how to mix a dry martini the way he liked them. He would show me. He took a three-pint stainless steel jug, tipped in an entire bottle of gin, added a whole tray of ice cubes, a sliced lemon and a single capful of dry vermouth. Satisfied, he returned to the sitting-room, plonked it in front of him, and began to smoke. At the end of the evening the ash tray was full and the jug empty.

Like many people who spend a lot of time living in other people's houses, he was adept at ensuring his own comfort.

At the end of a small dinner party, for example, he saw that his own glass was empty and so was the wine bottle. With one gracious gesture, he swept up my father's full glass, bade a cheery goodnight to all, and disappeared upstairs.

Another mealtime, he told us this story. The fashionable drug of the day was LSD, and he and his partner Chester Kaliman felt they should try the experience. They invited a doctor friend round one morning to administer it in their New York apartment. After an hour or so, nothing had happened, so they decided to go out for a meal at the diner round the corner. Suddenly Auden saw through the window his mailman, apparently performing an elaborate dance on the sidewalk. This was clearly the expected hallucination, so they rushed back home, where again nothing happened. Next day, the mailman knocked on their door. 'Hey, Mr Auden, I had this parcel for you yesterday. I saw you in the diner, and I waved at you a long time, but you looked right through me.'

His last day was a Sunday. I was the first member of our family up, and discovered him in the sitting-room, with a piece of greaseproof paper he'd found in the kitchen, carefully tracing the grid from the Observer crossword, so he could solve it without spoiling the puzzle for anyone else. It was a terrifically thoughtful gesture, though rather poignant too – here was a man who knew that his hospitality depended on his not leaving real or metaphorical footprints on the carpet or visiting minor inconveniences on his hosts, someone who was, for much of his life, dependent on the kindness of strangers.

SIMON HOGGART

Christopher Hamilton recalls his stay
as a wayward guest in the Commons

Pimm's on the House

One day, early in 1980, a dishevelled economic migrant wandered into the House of Commons. He squatted there for ten months in luxurious accommodation overlooking the Embankment and Westminster Bridge.

Mobile telephones had yet to make their mark. The corridors of power teemed with people of real character. Many were highly-educated and some were larger than life. Nobody was 'on message' and the place reeked of sex. Though cross-party friendships abounded, the only party this refugee had anything to do with involved industrial quantities of Pimm's.

The single dark shadow cast over the House came from the death of Airey Neave, whose car had been blown to pieces on a ramp leading out of the underground car park. Sinister icons, in the form of long poles with mirrors on the end, emerged to remind us that things had somehow changed forever, as policemen searched under cars for IRA bombs.

I had come from Florence on the tail of a financial mishap involving a Range Rover, some trailer-loads of wine and a very large overdraft. Homeless and with few friends in London at the time, I clutched at straws. The last of these was laid on the long-suffering back of the Assistant Serjeant-at-Arms of the House of Commons, whose offspring were childhood friends of mine. What was there to lose? I picked up the telephone and was put through to the Commander, and he made the fatal error of inviting me to stay in one of his spare rooms for what he called 'the duration'.

His apartments overlooked Westminster Bridge on one side, Speaker's Court and the rear windows of the Speaker's own magnificent riverside accommodation on the other. The rooms were large and redolent of Pugin, polish and gin. The length of green carpet running from the bathroom to the lift and front door could have graced the main runway at Fairford.

The Serjeant-at-Arms's Department is staffed by ex-servicemen and its role was to ensure supplies of everything from stationery to lavatory paper and ... security. It gave off an air of permanence, as 'here today and gone tomorrow' politicians sluiced past to left and right. The Commander had been a submariner during the war, and an exceptionally brave and decorated one at that. Among other acts of derring-do, he had surfaced his badly depth-charged vessel, engaged a German surface ship, then rammed and taken it. He was incisive and kind, but would never discuss his war. From wounds received at the time he developed severe arthritis, for which he took gin in naval measures in his wood-panelled wardroom until, finally incapable of speech, he would set sail on a 'rolling patrol'. He was good at his job and seldom returned without a 'kill'.

Equipped with a House of Commons pass, I had access to all floors except for that immediately below us. This contained the PM's offices and provided the Commander with a short-cut to the Chamber where, to my great surprise, he would perform faultlessly (if speechlessly), the arcane and complicated choreography of ceremonial duties required by his office.

The Commander was a model of sobriety when compared with some of the elected members he had, from time to time, to chastise. When dressing for the Chamber in black coat and breeches he chose Polly Peck sheer one-size tights over stockings, but stopped short of fish-nets – unlike a retired admiral of my acquaintance who would regularly wear them to church in Dorset when he read the lesson.

Mrs Commander, a stout woman from South Wales, was one of those big-hearted hangers and floggers. Had she been let loose in the Chamber, Welsh affairs would have been tidied up in a matter of minutes. And God help Ron Davies, had he been around at the time. Extraordinarily kind to almost everyone she met, Mrs Commander's politics did not always converge with those of her husband. He was surprisingly liberal – to a fault on some issues – but he came to heel on others. Among his closest cross-party allies was Mr Callaghan's Chief Whip. But Stalinism was still only a memory, and both major parties could still field alternatives to their leaders.

These were intoxicating times. Around the time of Mr Carter's failed attempt to rescue hostages from Tehran, I smuggled an Iranian girl into the flat and deflowered her (she said) on the Commanders' marital bed. The Commander knew of this debriefing almost immediately, so our subsequent interview was a sticky one. Another conquest had blue hair – leaving stains that were harder to explain, even during the ascendancy of She Who Must Be Obeyed. Another, who is now married to a celebrity, must remain nameless, if only because the encounter did not come up to her expectations. True, I was dishevelled, but no more so than Michael Foot. I behaved appallingly, but at least I could not be 'named' by the Speaker.

Daily life was studded with peculiar- ities. An ex-Chief Petty Officer came weekly to polish the Commander's sword. His was a busy day as he padded round both Houses putting a final buff on Wilkinson's finest steel. The Commander's blade was unusual of its kind in being razor sharp. Other members of the Serjeant-at-Arms's Department were billeted in the clock tower ,where one hears more of the clock mechanism than of the bells. Even where I slept, the bongs were no louder than they are on News at Ten. Far more intrusive was the tumble drier in its Pugin and green-carpet lair as Olga the maid brought in washing 24 hours a day, and muttered to herself in Russian.

Monitors in the corner of the sitting-room and in the kitchen displayed details of whatever business was in hand downstairs in the Chamber. The sound of debates in progress was nearly always low, or off, except during Welsh Questions, when Mrs Commander would turn up the volume and join in, bellowing unheard, gin in hand, at unseen tormentors in the Chamber below.

When dressing in black coat and breeches, the Commander chose Polly Peck tights over stockings, stopping short of fish-nets

Nearly all the furniture in the apartment belonged to the Property Services Agency. It was suited to the task, but only just. Years later, during Mr Major's time, and on a wobbly post-prandial visit to an office belonging to the Foreign Secretary (Mr Hurd was out), I looked down from his window into the garden of Number 10 and saw the most hideous wicker peacock throne. When I asked a Foreign Office functionary if this too was PSA furniture, I was assured that it was not: not even the PSA would entertain anything so monstrous. It was Norma's, he sniffed, through and through.

There was little to buy in the House of Commons apart from cheap cigarettes, booze, chocolates and votes. During the week one could shop at Strutton Ground market or at the Army and Navy Stores in Victoria Street. But at weekends it would have been possible to starve had the Commander not laid in supplies delivered weekly by messenger.

I found the authorities in the Palace of Westminster flexible, experienced and kind. One day, the Police Room called to ask if I knew a certain Mr X, who claimed to be a bailiff to the High Court delivering a writ to me. They were flying thick and fast at the time, but I replied that I had never heard of the

man. The sergeant was perplexed. He knew most of those bailiffs who came on a daily basis to present Members of Parliament with bankruptcy papers, paternity summonses, divorce petitions, orders concerning fraud, cottaging, etc. He agreed that the man might well be an impostor. So we had him locked up in the Police Room cells for the rest of the day while 'enquiries' were made.

I had been temporarily teetotal for all this time, and my celebratory 'falling-off-the-wagon' Pimm's party at the House of Commons was a recipe for disaster. It was held in the Commander's accommodation while he and Mrs Commander were holding a gin-fest of their own somewhere in the country. Though numbers were taken and the vehicles were checked for bombs, I should not have prevailed upon the police, so soon post-Airey Neave, to bend the rules and allow cars to be parked around part of a clockwise circuit between the two main gates. I can still remember the difficulty my guests found in driving out again, and the damage caused to and by their vehicles.

Fruit was dutifully chopped up by Olga, ice, borage and mint were procured but, forever unwilling to read instructions, I composed the drink as I saw fit at the time: two parts of gin to one of Pimm's and then with no more than a dash of lemonade added. My guests, though served large measures from the outset, behaved well at first. Then they were shown around deserted parts of the Palace, before having their pint mugs charged again, and again. Suddenly, someone suggested we should play 'Badgers'. From this point on, everything is a blur – even 22 years later. All I can remember is police officers removing us from Speaker's Green where, on all fours, we had set off the alarms.

Had such a Pimm's moment taken place today, there could have been a bloodbath – 'He was waving a bottle, we thought it was a petrol bomb, so we opened fire.' Mind you, when you take my Pimm's recipe into consideration, the police would have a point. But it marked a turning point. As the Commander pointed out to me the following Monday, by arcane powers still held by the Serjeant-at-Arms, he could have had me incarcerated in the Tower of London.

It occurred fleetingly that this could be a good plan, but I was distracted by the way he kept fingering his sword. ◉

'You white folk hate us, and we hate you motherf***ers back!' the comedian screamed. The predominantly African-American audience howled with laughter. The sole white couple in the comedy club grinned defiantly.

'Look me in the eye! Go on! Dare to look me in the eye and tell me how much you hate us niggers!'

The white man threw back his head and guffawed. The woman next to me collapsed on my shoulder, shaking with mirth. I fixed a grotesquely false grin on my face and prayed to become invisible. If l were picked out as an object of ridicule by the comedian I would most certainly be subjected to hours of mocking torture. The comedian's first question would be details of my 'ethnic background'. The answer would produce a diatribe of hatred amid hysterical laughter. My voice would generate sneering mirth as the comedian would explain, in vicious detail, his hatred of the 'Briddish'.

The word 'hate' should have given you a clue to where I was – South Florida – the closest place to hell on earth. This ghastly comedy club was the horrific climax of my awful holiday.

'And what are you, motherf***er?' demanded the comedian, eyes aflame, pointing to a young attractive woman.

'I'm Cuban.'

'Cuban! Come on the boat with the Haitians and the Guatemalatians and the Mexicans so you can work for nothing and take our jobs! Why didn't someone sink your boat and drown y'all? You hate us as much as the white folks do, but don't think we're afraid of you, sister!' Loud cheers rent the air. I frowned momentarily into my lemonade.

'Hey, you! Miss Misery! You with the face like an accident on its way to heaven!' The comedian's long, bony finger and the faces of the audience were pointing towards me. I desperately tried to attempt a fake smile, but, alas, my face muscles had paralysed in terror.

'Where you from? You look mix race and mix up.'

'If l were governor of Florida,' I thought, as I stared in mute horror, 'I would ban clubs such as this one.' Florida is hate-filled enough as it is – we all know about the black vote being stolen during the past election – without horrible comedians prodding their pitchforks into the furnace of unpleasantness.

Zenga Longmore went to Florida, where everything is done to excess. She has a few suggestions for the Governor

Largely unpleasant

I would not be a very popular governor because I would also ban cars. Unless one is prepared to face certain death, it is advisable not to walk in the part of West Palm Beach where I stayed. The green light lasted for five seconds before giant cars accelerated all around me as I ran screaming across ten-lane motorways.

Walkers are the great Unmentionable, the most despised things human beings can be – poor. A trip to a chemist to buy headache pills involves a five-mile walk in the cruel heat, and there is no one around to ask for directions. The shops along the motorways are violently huge and hideous.

How beautiful Florida must once have been, with its palms, lush flowers and tropical sun. Now, giant concrete malls rise from the ground; Goya-esque spectres shimmering in the polluted air. Perhaps the ugliness of the surroundings enforces an ugliness of feeling. All the hard, lowpaid work appears to be done by Latin and Central Americans, yet the wealthier African and European Americans despise them because they 'come over to this country and do all the work'. I was repeatedly to hear this senseless logic throughout my ten tortuous days in Florida.

How had I got into this mess? What was I doing in Florida? Well, I am a doting parent, so when my teenage daughter Omalara and my equally deluded seven-year-old niece insisted I take them to Florida, what could I do but dote? Omalara had a friend who moved to West Palm Beach and my niece loved the films of Walt Disney. I myself admired the writings of the Florida novelist Zora Neale Hurston, whose home in Polk County has now been taken over by Disneyland.

Abolishing the entire Disney Corporation would cause me intense pleasure. After gobbling up the whole of Orlando, Disney has belched out

ILLUSTRATION BY M H JEEVES

horrific, overpriced plastic theme parks. We queued for ninety minutes in the sweltering heat for the dubious pleasure of meeting a perspiring man in a Goofy mask.

Finally, Governor Zenga would force the Floridians to say 'So long, buddy' to the numerous All You Can Eat For $10 restaurants. This last enforcement might cause a riot, but fortunately the rioters would be too fat to manage the petrol bombs. The memory of witnessing those Floridians wedged into specially crafted double chairs eating all they could is making me feel too queasy to continue.

Gargantuan families squeezed painfully out of their cars and waddled into the 'All You Can Eats'. Fathers and mothers were often in wheelchairs, having been rendered disabled by their appetites. I have heard it said that America's excess resembles the last days of the Roman Empire; both are empires built on slavery, but at least the Romans, with their mosaics and temples, had a respect for beauty, and surely the Civitas Roman us could not have been so slow and blubbery.

Meanwhile, back at the Comedy club. 'Hey, you, sister! Bitch!' the comedian howled, hardly audible above the bellows of applause. 'I said where you from? You look like one of them and I HATE them – Guatemaliatians!' (Loud cheers.)

I may be a cowardy-custard, but no one can accuse me of being a dull-witted cowardy-custard. Pretending that my mirth was so overwhelming as to cause complete helplessness, I collapsed on the table and continued to shake my entire upper body until the pleas of the comedian to know where I was from became too tedious to pursue.

If only I had heeded the advice of my brother Roy: 'If you want to queue up for hours to see people who look like dogs, go to Worthing Pier.' I'm not quite sure what Roy meant either, but it makes more sense than a holiday in Florida. ⑩

The word 'hate' should have given you a clue to where I was – South Florida, the closest place to hell on earth

'...and you must be Sleazy!'

'That's the financial district'

'I thought we could freeze it...'

John Amis has known the artist John Craxton – who he now describes as an 'elderly schoolboy' – since the Forties. What was it that first drew Craxton to his beloved Greece?

The artist's eye

I f it were not for an unsightly snaggle-tooth, John Craxton would seem to be more of an elderly schoolboy than an oldie (born 1922). He is much as I remember him in the Forties, when one evening after a concert and a drink or three, John and Lucian (as in Freud) climbed a lamppost in Piccadilly. I stayed on terra firma anxiously on the qui vive for any rozzers wanting to have a word with us.

The two painters were close in those days, sharing studio space paid for by generous, rich Peter Watson (erstwhile Horizon angel). But Johnny's first exhibition was solo at the Leicester Gallery, director Oliver Brown. In the Forties there were quite a few brushmen shooting up (in the old sense): Minton, Vaughan, Ayrton, Colquhoun and McBride ('Said Colquhoun to McBride: there's a position we've not tried' began the limerick). What impressed me and many others at the time was the 1944 anthology called The Poet's Eye with superb cuts by John. Geoffrey Grigson had the nous and clout to commission JC to adorn his excellent collection of poems and prose on visionary themes. Great success.

In that same year John went drawing in Pembrokeshire with Graham

Sutherland and his wife. John was particularly struck with the quality of light and took note of Graham saying that perhaps his younger colleague should go to Greece where the light was similar. Sutherland was quite an influence, but the major one was Palmer. JC says he will never forget the electric shock he received when Peter Watson thrust into his hand his first sighting of a reproduction of a Samuel Palmer. At once he saw how to integrate a human figure into a pastoral landscape. There is drama in C's work but usually, as with Palmer, there is that feeling of well-being, of serendipity: sheer joy is the reaction

Sheer joy is the reaction of the viewer to Craxton's work

of the viewer. Of course, life can be grim but, with any luck, it also contains moments of pleasure, of serenity, even ecstasy; there is no sentimentality in Craxton's work but something of Palmer's entrancing and satisfying perception of nature by means of design, colour, proportion and exuberant ingenuity.

Feelings like that are also present in music, a potent feature in Craxton's life. Not surprising, since there was much of it in the Hampstead house where John was brought up and where he still lives when in England. Father Harold was a pianist, especially famous as an accompanist; he was one of the first on this side of the Channel to play the music of Debussy. Mrs C was Essie, gracious, decorative, a lovely person. Three brothers, but it was sister Janet that John felt closest to. She was a distinguished oboist, and there was no person in the music world more respected and loved. So the house was full of music, and is now full of John's paintings. A trust ensures that the big studio is available to singers and instrumentalists for rehearsals and

Landscape, Hydra, **1960–61**

concerts. John paints upstairs and lives happily with Richard, his partner of many years, a collector and purveyor of books and objets d'art.

Trouble above the belt kept Craxton out of World War Two; after the war ended he followed Sutherland's hint and went to Greece, falling in love with the country, the lifestyle and the light; by now he has spent half his life there. One day Frederick Ashton telephoned with the suggestion that Craxton might do the décor for his production of Ravel's ballet Daphnis and Chloé. Great success: a Daphnis of clean lines and clear colour, sets and costumes, no abstractions, no wishy-washiness.

Later came artwork for Stravinsky's Apollo. Exhibitions have taken place every two or three years, although I detect recently a certain reluctance on the painter's part to sell, a tendency that steadily puts the price up. So there must be many exhilarating canvases waiting to see the light of day and the delight of viewers.

John says he would like to travel more but he is too busy in London painting every day. But even while he is painting music is piped through his earphones.

He doesn't go out much for music but loves it when the Nash Ensemble comes to the studio to rehearse. He used to spend a lot of time on his beloved motorbike but a bad knee has cut that down. He also has to go to the doctor for trouble below the belt, but Richard says he doesn't listen much to medical advice. He reads a lot, serious books and Private Eye. University Challenge is a favourite. But painting is what makes John Craxton tick; painting, not promoting it. He never seeks publicity or recognition. He just paints. It's a necessity.

And his pleasure. And ours. 𝕀

Detail from *The Poet's Eye*, 1944

First the smokers, then the drinkers

The first of July 2007 was the day on which smoking in church was banned by law. At least, it was in England. For all I know, the Scots may still be allowed to light up during the sermon, and Welsh churchwardens may puff their pipes in the pews at the back while they discuss the price of leeks.

If I were a vicar, I would not just put up the statutory notice; I would get the ladies of the parish to work me a tapestry which set it out in proper form: 'Whereas the grievous fin of fmoaking, being an invention of Beelzebub to entrap the fouls of the unwary, hath of recent years monftroufly increafed, ye who enter into this place are to defift therefrom, under the pains and penalties fet out hereunder. James 4:7.'

That, as they say, should do the business, until such time as a further notice is required, as part of what the *Times* calls a coming 'crackdown on middle-class wine-drinkers'. Warnings of the evil of alcohol are expected to go up in all public places where drink is taken.

For this the wording is readily to hand in the form of a tablet set into the wall of the old vicarage in the parish of Kirdford in Sussex. Headed 'Degredation of Drunkenness', it reads: 'There is no sin which doth more deface God's image than drunkenness. It is the shame of nature, the extinguisher of reason, the shipwreck of chastity and the murder of conscience. The cup kills more than the cannon.'

I see myself peacefully sitting in the pub when the drink police arrive

This should do nicely not just for churches but for public houses as part of the Government campaign to turn the pubs of England into places where you are forbidden to smoke and strongly discouraged from drinking.

My own disreputable career as a middle-class drinker began at Oxford, where I went in 1948, at a time when there were still undergraduates who had been in the war. In those days there was a rule that we might not go into public houses. Now you can, if you feel like it, tell a man who has come through El Alamein that he cannot have a pint in a pub when he wants to. You can do it, but it does not work, as such men take no notice. Thus some ex-Squadron Leader would be quietly sipping bitter alongside some former Brigade Major at the bar of The Bear, when in would come the proctors' Bulldogs, as the bowler-hatted university police were called.

'Are you a member of this university, sir?'

'Yes I am.'

'Your college, sir?'

'Trinity.'

'Your name, sir?'

'Brown.'

Then these two would be hauled before the proctors and fined, I think, three pounds.

I am expecting similar scenes when the Great Crackdown starts. I see myself sitting peacefully in the Rose and Crown, when in come the drink police, hot on the heels of the smoke police.

'Is that a glass I see before you, sir?'

'It is.'

'Did it contain alcoholic liquor?'

'It did, till I emptied it.'

'Your name and postcode, sir?'

Then I shall be breathalysed, and later fined for drinking more than the government thinks good for me, and endangering the fabric of the NHS.

House Husbandry
with Giles Wood

If you thought country life was all cosy Agas, crackling log fires and close-knit communities, think again...

'Just say no!' I shout at my wife Mary as the telephone rings. It's Festive Season all year round in this neck of the woods and people are permanently issuing invitations. Mary is a gregarious creature who welcomes the overtures. I, by contrast, identify more with the ponies in a nearby field. They have got their backs to the east wind and are standing three deep, their heads down, embedded in a blackthorn thicket.

It is impossible to get our Wiltshire cottage up to temperature when the east wind blows. Some years ago the powers that be told us that asthma was caused by house-dust mites which thrive in modern, hermetically-sealed, triple-glazed homes. Here at last was something we were doing right. Sometimes the cottage resembles nothing so much as a giant Aeolian harp as the draughts gust through it, starting on one note and rising a full six tones before falling again. Draughts make life difficult for mites and humans alike. Now the powers that be are telling us to seal them up to combat climate change.

But no need, I say. I can achieve a reasonable body temperature by wrapping up and wedging myself into a Parker Knoll, just to the left of the cold jet stream drawn in through the sitting-room door. .

I keep telling Mary that the secret of staying warm in a cottage is not to move from room to room but to stay put – but she is ill-suited to hamlet life in a fridge.

'Any house is warmer than ours,' she wails. Even more reason for her eagerness to socialise so promiscuously amongst the Aga-owning classes. I would unwedge myself from my Parker Knoll if I thought that intellectual stimulation might accrue, but surely I can find more of that sitting in my armchair with a good book than I could on the Aga circuit?

> 'You'd be better off dead,' my wife said the other day. 'At least that way you could give something back to the demineralised fields'

'I will go out,' I tell Mary, 'If you can assure me that amongst the guests would be either the Gaia hypothesist James Lovelock, the composer Michael Berkeley or the biologist E O Wilson. Even A N Wilson would do.'

One thing has changed since Richard Jefferies wrote *Toilers of the Field* back in 1892 . There are no toilers in the field any more, nor field-faring women, the subject of another of his essays. Instead I look out onto a visual irritant in the distance. A handy pair of field glasses reveals a demented quad bike beetling across the sepia pasture. A call to the farm office reveals the toiler is spreading industrial-strength slug pellets of the type unavailable to the amateur gardener.

Yet the view from the back window shows my own garden, which is not over-tidy, is full of the birds that co-existed alongside farming up until 50 years ago.

The happiest moments come when Mary spots a bird which I can identify for her. Yesterday it was a redwing. Despite my patient tutelage, she can still only reliably identify seagulls and robins, yet her simple request for information is a positive sign. It offers a flicker of hope that we might have something in common after all.

When, as a painter between commissions, I am in this immobile condition, Mary becomes shrewish. 'You would be better off dead,' she said the other day. 'At least that way you could give something back to the demineralised fields.' But I don't take it personally.

As Richard Jefferies, who visited our village in the 19th century, noted in *Field-Faring Women*, 'The pressure of hard circumstances and the endless battle with poverty, render men and women both callous to others' feelings.'

One social event I did attend was a small local rough shoot. We needed something for the pot. Dressed as Michelin Man I was unable to swing the gun to make that vital connection with my target. Nevertheless, the one commodity I have in plenty is time. So I brought back three brace of pheasant because the metropolitan guns were short of time and there was no-one available for plucking and drawing.

I got one from the freezer and roasted it for Mary last night. 'The hunter gatherer provides,' I beamed. 'I don't know about hunting but you're certainly a gatherer,' she said. 🜋

OWNING gold can seem like an impossible dream. But there are solutions for everyone – even during these uncertain times. Throughout history, gold has been used as a means of portfolio diversification. And since 2014, Rosland has helped clients all over the UK achieve financial security through gold.

A GOLDEN LEGACY

We all need to prepare for the future, to ensure our loved ones are protected when the time is right. In 2022's autumn budget, the UK government made the decision to cut the threshold for paying capital gains tax from £12,300 to £6,000 in 2023, and it will be cut again to £3,000 in 2024. Many of Rosland's coins are capital gains tax FREE (as well as VAT free), meaning you can pass them on to your loved ones safe in the knowledge that they won't have to pay a single penny in tax.

INSIGHT & EXPERTISE

To ensure its validity, it is vital to know where your gold comes from. Rosland works directly with the world's finest mints to source the very best coins for their clients, many of which are legal tender. Rosland's extensive collection includes a diverse range of commemorative, limited-edition and rare coins – even treasure from the bottom of the ocean! Whenever their specialists find a coin they think you'll love, your account manager will be in touch to ensure you are the first to know about it.

GRADED COIN SPECIALISTS

Rosland are the industry specialists in graded coins. One of the most

Want to protect your wealth from the invisible enemy that is inflation? Then you need a specialist in precious gold coins...

DISCOVER THE TAX ADVANTAGES OF GOLD COINS
VAT has been abolished on gold coins of a certain purity, while British legal tender coins are exempt from Capital Gains Tax

ROSLAND GOLD.CO.UK

important features of a coin - and key to its value - is its condition. Buying graded coins ensures maximum security, value and liquidity.

GET YOUR FREE GOLD GUIDE

From its early uses in ancient Egypt to its pivotal role in modern technology and medicine, discover everything you need to know about this fascinating metal with your free copy of **The Rosland Book of Gold**. This comprehensive guide is filled

with stories, trivia, industry insight – everything you need to know before starting your very own gold portfolio.

PROTECT YOUR WEALTH NOW

Call Rosland's gold experts now for your free copy of their guide to gold, and discover the safe, professional and enjoyable way to protect your wealth from the invisible enemy of inflation.

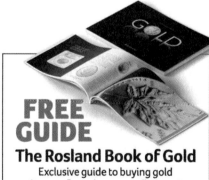

Interview

Katharine Whitehorn

The 'insufficiently dainty' writer and columnist talks to
Melanie McFadyean about widowhood, being an agony aunt
and why an unhappy childhood is good for you

Reading *Selective Memory*, Katharine Whitehorn's autobiography is like spending a few hours in her company. She writes as she speaks, with wit, ease and honesty, and she never fails to communicate – possibly the secret of her success as a journalist. Never sententious, self-serving or sentimental, what comes through is a combination of good sense, humour, liberalism and the old fashioned decency. In her book, you breeze and bluster through her long and busy life and discover how she survived the rough and bleak times – her latest triumph being surviving widowhood after the death of her beloved husband of 45 years, the thriller writer Gavin Lyall.

She has a moment, after his death, when she sees the 'the mudflats of the future stretched endlessly ahead... real widowhood began.' But she doesn't vanish into the mudflats. She finds her way back, regains her zest for life, and gets back on the road, travelling, working and dispensing advice. 'Many unhappy people,' she says, 'are like flies buzzing endlessly at the glass when there's an open window a foot away.'

Whitehorn currently fields crises as *Saga*'s agony aunt while popping up on a regular basis in other magazines and newspapers, but a quick run through her 47-year-old career reveals that crooked journey many journalists go on before finding their niche.

We all start somewhere and she started on *Home Notes*, which, according to Whitehorn, was 'printed on loo paper' and for which she subedited allegedly true-life stories. When she joined *Picture Post* in 1956, she was where she wanted to be.

It all fell into place 'because I so liked an unsettled life'. She loved it, never knowing whether she'd be in Paris covering the shows or posing for Bert Hardy as a lonely girl in London at

Katharine Whitehorn (1928-2021) – 'an early love life replete with cads'

Waterloo station. She loved the late-night bars, the camaraderie, the gossip.

After an interestingly colourful love life, replete with cads, heartbreakers, 'a highly enriching *amitié amoureuse*' and successfully resisted adulterous urges (all touched upon in her autobiography), she met Gavin, then a fellow journalist on the *Picture Post*. An early supporter of feminism before the movement took off, she nevertheless says the day she

had her first son was the 'single happiest day of my life', and remembers looking down from a grassy bank at Gavin, in their boat Simpkin, and thinking, 'There is all my happiness.'

From *Picture Post* she went to *Woman's Own*, but was sacked for 'not writing sufficiently dainty copy'.

After a brief spell teaching in a charm school for young housewives, she joined the *Spectator*, where she

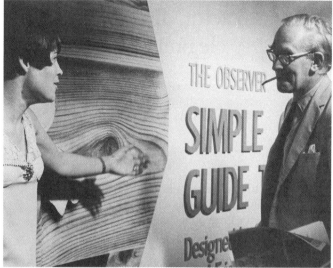

Above left: Bert Hardy's photo of Whitehorn for a *Picture Post* article, 'Lonely in London'. Above right: with George Seddon, her editor at the *Observer*

wrote a column, the forerunner to the *Observer* column which was later to make her one of the UK's most famous journalists and a household name to a generation of readers.

As a star columnist on the *Observer*, under its highly innovative features editor, George Seddon, she was the first woman in British journalism to make a success of writing about things that matter in every day life.

Thirty-six years later, the column was axed. Will Hutton, the then editor, gave her the news over lunch. 'Will poured drink into me and said, "We want to stop the column." He felt I'd been going on too long and he wanted a new look. He said, "I want you much more in the loop doing features." I believed it, but nobody else did.'

The features writing went pear-shaped when two big pieces appeared under headlines that appalled her. In the autobiography, she says her trouble at the *Observer* was due to Hutton's new young deputy, Jocelyn Targett, who, she writes, 'effectively ran the show'. She doesn't go into detail, and I wondered why. 'The libel lawyer took out most of what I said about Jocelyn Targett,' she replied with a wry smile.

'Will Hutton is much more of a writer and visionary than a natural editor [and] so left a great deal of the normal editing to Targett, whose first act was to discontinue the two most popular columnists, John Naughton and me.'

There were then four 'nasty' months before she resigned in the spring of 1997. The catalyst came when she asked when a piece about to miss its moment was

going to be used. The features editor, whose name she says she has mercifully forgotten, replied tetchily that she had 24 other freelancers all asking the same question. At that moment, Whitehorn says she thought, 'What the blazes was I doing waiting for this chit to tell me when my piece would be used? It was the last straw. The moment to go.' She resigned. She didn't know until later 'that there was a building-wide row about discontinuing my column.'

Instead of descending into the rancour and gloom of the disgruntled former employee in her twilight years, she says, 'The six months before were so miserable that the relief when I had finally gone was fantastic.' She was then invited to do *Saga*'s agony column and has been doing it ever since.

Dozens of columnists have followed in Whitethorn's tracks, only a few of them with comparable skill. She thinks a common mistake is to imagine that all that's needed is 'mildly amusing chat', whereas she made sure her columns were about something more than 'how some fancy bachelor deals with his dustbins'. She would 'take an

> '**Many unhappy people are like flies buzzing endlessly at the glass when there's an open window a foot away**'

event or trend or book or something and extrapolate from it, or a personal thing that led into a general thought, so that it wasn't just lifestyle, full stop.'

Whitehorn now has two sons, a grandchild and a step grandchild. Where she found the time to be Rector of St Andrew's, on the boards of BAA, the Nationwide Building Society and the Royal Society of Medicine, as well as an active and founding member of the UK arm of the International Women's Forum, God only knows.

What is it that has enabled her to survive? 'I've had good luck almost all the way. I've been incredibly lucky, because bad things have turned into good things.' Like not being able to marry Colin, a man who left her in her twenties after a passionate affair, which led to her marrying Gavin, a much better thing in every way.

Any suggestion that it is her spirit and lust for life that made this luck come her way is swept aside.

'A possible key to me is that, having had an unhappy childhood, I have always been much more conscious of being happy and lucky because of those awful years when I had no friends. I now have masses and am still astonished and delighted people want to be my friend.' When times were rough, she didn't go in for letting it all hang out. In her book she says she 'kept the show on the road and thought that was what mattered'.

'One just bloody well got on with it,' she told me, as she offered me coffee – or perhaps something stronger, and bugger the time of day. ◐

Veteran actor, director and writer *Patrick Garland* remembers the
elegant but foul-mouthed actress Coral Browne

A State of Grace

Coral Browne, a very devout Roman Catholic, was emerging from the Brompton Oratory one Sunday morning when she saw her great friend Charles Gray (famous for playing Ernst Stavro Blofeld with his white Persian cat in three *James Bond* films) advancing up the steps of the Oratory with a salacious glint in his eye. Out of the corner of her mouth, she hissed: 'Fuck off, Charles, I'm in a State of Grace.'

Coral was a wonderful-looking woman all her life, very smart, very much in tune with the appearance of leading ladies of the day. She spoke with a distinct Australian accent, but not on the stage. A grande dame, whose diction was perfect, she was, for a time, kept by a very distinguished producer of the 1930s called Firth Shepherd. 'Firth is my Shepherd, I'll not want,' she said of his generosity. She had a brilliant career, starred frequently in the West End, and was much loved by her friends, although her tongue could be somewhat acerbic. Alec McCowen told me that when he was asked to play Count Almaviva at the Old Vic in Beaumarchais' *Marriage of Figaro*, he rang Coral for her opinion. 'I wouldn't touch it with a barge pole, dear. Even when it opened in the 18th century, it never worked as a straight play and they had to turn it into a musical!'

She successfully married money,

Effing chic: Coral Browne in 1965

had a great sense of style and dressed impeccably. When she was playing Mrs Erlynne in *Lady Windermere's Fan*, she was presented with a red dress designed by Cecil Beaton, which was very much alien to her colouring. 'I can't wear this, Cecil,' she said to the legendary designer of *My Fair Lady*, 'I look like a fire hydrant and dogs will come up in the street and pee on me.'

On one occasion she hailed a taxi and a rather smart looking English gent in a Savile Row suit and black bowler hat, not seeing her, came in from the opposite door. A string of invective poured out as she took charge of the car. 'Sorry Guv'nor, looks like I'm already hired to this lady,' said the taxi driver. 'What lady?' asked the highly indignant gentleman. 'This f***ing lady,' was Coral's reply.

She generally got on well with her fellow actors, but guarded her position very zealously. On one occasion she was

working in a distinguished comedy with Ernest Thesiger, a wonderful character actor. He held a cherished position in the hearts of the younger actors of those days, because he belonged, in diction and posture, to the old school.

Towards the end of his life, Ernest, who had frequently played the dashing young men in Oscar Wilde's plays, generally played butlers, but always with great distinction. As somebody once said of him, when he played a butler, Ernest was much grander than any member of the aristocracy on stage. But he could be distracting, and that was something Coral Browne could never put up with. During her principal scene, she had been aware that, behind her, Ernest was indulging in comic business while he cleared away the champagne glasses and the bottle in its bucket, and by his expressions of distaste was creating a neat little harvest of giggles for himself which took away the focus from the

> 'I can't wear this, Cecil,' she said to the legendary designer of *My Fair Lady*, 'I look like a fire hydrant and dogs will come up in the street and pee on me'

main action. Coral, at the curtain call, murmured to Ernest: 'Would you care for a gin and tonic, dear?' He duly went up to her dressing room, and with a large gin in his hand, expressed himself shocked when Coral told him that she might not be performing next week. 'Oh, Coral,' he said with great concern (he counted himself a close friend), 'I hope you haven't got anything dangerously wrong with you?' 'No,' said Coral lightly, 'It's nothing too complicated, but I've got to go into hospital for a little minor surgery. It's not too serious. I'm just having eyes sewn into the back of my f***ing head.'

Her fellow Australian, Charles Osborne, formerly the Secretary of the Arts Council, told me he was travelling in a taxi to a theatre – he was drama critic of the *Daily Telegraph* at the time – and was getting off at the Globe and paying the taxi cab when the driver took up a conversation with him. 'I had one of those very famous actresses in the back of my cab the other day,' he said. 'Edith Evans? Sybil Thorndike?' said Charles Osborne helpfully. 'No, no, no,' said the taxi driver. 'No, you know her – very well turned out woman.' 'Margaret Leighton? Or maybe it was Maggie Smith?' he said. 'No,' said the taxi driver. 'No, it wasn't none of them. She was standing there, effing and blinding, and swearing like a trooper.' Charles didn't hesitate. 'Oh, I know who you mean,' he said. 'Coral Browne.' ◍

On the dance floor in *Let George Do It* (1940)

'Well, okay, but only if it advances the plot'

Poop-poop!
100 years of Mr Toad

The Wind in the Willows has given enormous pleasure to generations of readers of all ages. *Richard Ingrams* celebrates its centenary and looks at the background of author Kenneth Grahame

Kenneth Grahame 1912 drawn by John S Sargent

For a fictional all-male group of Thames Valley idlers, stemming from the imagination of a senior Bank of England official, to survive from the Edwardian age into the politically-correct world of the 21st century is an extraordinary achievement. But that is what they have done – Mole, Ratty, Badger and Toad, the cast of *The Wind in the Willows*, first published in 1908.

Not only have they survived, they have flourished through a series of editions selling thousands upon thousands of copies, not to mention stage shows and films. And they will still be here, I predict, when Harry Potter is forgotten.

Like many of the world's bestsellers, *The Wind in the Willows* was turned down by at least one publisher and received a fairly lukewarm reception from the critics when it was eventually published. 'As a contribution to natural history,' the *Times*'s anonymous reviewer wrote, 'the work is negligible ... grown-up readers will find it monstrous and elusive.'

Seeking to explain the later success of the book, Grahame's biographer Peter Green claimed, rather too seriously, that 'Its symbolism embodies mankind's deepest and most ineradicable yearnings: the pastoral dream, the Golden

Age, the search for lost innocence.' None of that has much to do with Grahame's most famous creation, Mr Toad, who makes such a special appeal to children and without whom the book would be colourless and bland.

Toad is the archetypal boaster, megalomaniac and monster. He is Jeffrey Archer, Robert Maxwell, Alan Clark – but with one very important difference. He is, as Grahame intended him to be, a loveable figure and, in his way, a kind of hero. Significantly, at the end of the story, Mr Toad remains a free man when by rights he would have been recaptured and put back in prison. More importantly, he has no intention of mending his ways. 'Of course Toad never reformed,' Grahame once wrote. 'He was by nature incapable of it.'

Attempts have been made to trace the inspiration for Mr Toad, with many rather absurd theories put forward. Some claimed he was based on Horatio Bottomley, the Robert Maxwell of his day. Alan Bennett, who adapted *The Wind in the Willows* for the stage, even saw Grahame as an anti-semite and Toad a vicious caricature of a Jewish financier. More convincingly, it has been suggested that Toad was inspired in part by Grahame's only child, his son Alastair, for whom the book was originally composed in the form of bed-time stories. Spoiled and bumptious, Alastair showed Toad-like tendencies.

Grahame's relationship with the small boy was the only truly happy one he had. His mother died when he was only five. His father, Cunningham Grahame, a Scottish lawyer and an alcoholic, sent away his four children to be brought up by their grandmother in England. His wife Elspeth was hopelessly neurotic and, most tragically of all, Alastair, who had been born half-blind and had always been 'difficult', committed suicide on a railway line in Oxford when he was only 19.

Grahame's characters can be seen as creatures bred out of this unhappy background. They are all bachelors with a special love for their homes.

As a young man Grahame had had a recurring dream of a room of his own somewhere in London, a dream so vivid that he actually scoured the city for days in the hope of finding his room. 'A certain little room – very dear and familiar, sequestered in some corner of the more populous and roaring part of London – always the same feeling of a homecoming, the world shut out, of the idea of encasement.'

The story echoes the most powerful passage in the book, when Mole, walking through the snowy night with Rat, is suddenly overcome with homesickness: 'Now with a rush of old memories, how clearly it stood up before him in the darkness. Shabby indeed and small and poorly furnished, and yet his, the home he had been so happy to get back to after his day's walk. And the home had been happy with him, too, evidently and was missing him and wanted him back...'

Grahame never found his dream room in London. The nearest he came to the feeling of peace and security it promised was by writing his famous book – 'the world shut out' – and so finding not merely success, which he was uncomfortable with, but happiness of a sort and the 'encasement' that he craved. ◑

Illustrations by Inga Moore from the abridged version of Kenneth Grahame's The Wind in the Willows, *published by Walker Books, £25*

GRANNY ANNEXE

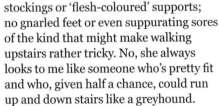

Virginia Ironside

Puttin' on the Ritz

Someone once said that 'beautiful young people are accidents of nature, but beautiful old people are works of art.' I rather like that. Indeed, I've often thought how true it is. When we're young, after all, we all look pretty good. Our skin blooms, our eyes are bright, and we can wear bin bags and torn jeans and still get away with it.

But when we're old we have to take more trouble. And because so few older people do take the trouble to look good, it's not difficult, with only the minimum of effort, to look vastly better than most of one's contemporaries. It's pretty easy, if you don't take care, to look like a vandalised 1950s community hall in Moss Side; but it only takes a bit of trouble and imagination and you can easily look like some glorious old ruin, such as Tintern Abbey.

There's no excuse to look invisible, as so many of my friends fear they do now they've reached sixty. In her poem, *Warning,* Jenny Joseph said that when she grew old she'd wear purple with 'red that doesn't go' and satin sandals. She would certainly stand out, but not in a good way. What's wrong with simply wearing outrageously fashionable clothes? Or putting feathers in your hair?

I've often wondered what it would be like to be one of those Old People Models. You find them on the covers of Bupa leaflets, or, sometimes, at the back of magazines like this. (Not, of course, that there is any other magazine like this. That is its strength).

These Bupa model couples nearly always wear identical windcheaters or whatever you call them these days. She has immaculate greying hair, set in a kind of casual, windswept style. He has masses of white hair which usually starts just above his eyebrows (he's not bald, oh dear me no; he's with Bupa!) and they're often standing on the deck of a

Old People Models set a good example to oldies who have 'let themselves go'

yacht or in some other affluent setting, sometimes even leaning on the rail. He is often pointing out to sea at some kind of illusionary future. And they've both got very silly smiles on their faces and you know why – it's because they both know that when their hips go, the operations will be paid for by Bupa.

Then there's the old lady who sits on a stairlift going up and down, up and down. She's frightfully well turned-out, with a white perm and a nice white cardigan. Look at her legs: no elasticated stockings or 'flesh-coloured' supports; no gnarled feet or even suppurating sores of the kind that might make walking upstairs rather tricky. No, she always looks to me like someone who's pretty fit and who, given half a chance, could run up and down stairs like a greyhound.

Then there's the woman with the fantastically good figure who is always about to step in to her walk-in bath. Not only does she have her make-up on but she's also wearing a one-piece bathing costume. Don't you think that's odd? I don't know about you, but I never have a bath in a bathing costume.

Finally, there's my favourite – the woman who's always to be found at the bottom of a long flight of stairs, sprawled on the carpet. I think she's posed by Mrs Hope, the famous Old Person Model. Her beautifully polished shoes are still on her feet, her stockings are unladdered, her nails unbroken and she hasn't a hair out of place as she clutches her panic button.

Of course these models are all frightfully unrealistic, but they do at least set a good example to oldies who have, in that dread phrase, 'let themselves go'. I'll never forget an old gentleman who used to live down the road. Every day he stood outside his house wearing a worn but charming pinstripe suit, a beautifully pressed shirt, a rose in his button hole, an immaculately knotted tie, and sparkling shoes. He also wore a hat which he removed when ladies passed. One day he crumpled up in the street and was taken away to a mortuary. But what a stylish guy!

Okay, in our own homes we can look like grubby blots on the landscapes from dawn to dusk. But we owe it not only to ourselves but to others to look, when we go out, as good as we possibly can. ◑

The Virginia Monologues: Twenty Reasons Why Growing Old Is Great (Fig Tree, £12.99)

Willy Field, a German Jewish refugee, survived Dachau and came to Britain in 1939. He didn't set foot on German soil again until 1945 – driving a Cromwell tank for his regiment, the 8th King's Royal Irish Hussars. Interview by *Melanie McFadyean*

Finding something good

Willy Field exudes warmth and good cheer; he is one of those rare people you feel you have known all your life even as you shake his hand on your first encounter – in my case on his doorstep in North London at the house he has shared with his wife Judy since 1954.

Thanks to historian Helen Fry's excellent biography *From Dachau to D Day*, I knew his story. In her book, Fry remarks on his lack of bitterness. But I was sceptical. How could someone who has been victim and witness of Nazi brutality not harbour bitterness somewhere in his soul?

Willy was living happily with his family in Bonn aged twelve when the horror begun. It was 1933 and the Nazis had just taken power. He remembers waking to the sound of hundreds of SA men marching and singing the Horst Wessel song.

A year later he saw the Nazis burning books and Jewish shops set on fire; he saw the body of his best friend, shot dead for making a remark about the Hitler Youth. He was thrown out of school for being Jewish. And then on Kristallnacht in November 1938 the Gestapo came for him. A hundred Jews were killed and some 25,000 were arrested and sent to concentration camps. Willy was taken to Dachau, where he experienced the prelude to the full-scale slaughter that was to come. On arrival the prisoners were forced to strip, were hosed down, and had their heads shaved. He saw people walk into the electrified barbed wire fence, choosing suicide rather than the cruelty and insanity of the camp's regime. When someone failed to appear for roll call, all were made to stand in freezing cold for 48 hours and fifty people died. Willy tried to prop up a fellow inmate but he collapsed and was taken away, never to be seen again.

His parents managed to get him a visa and a work permit for the UK, with which they bargained for his release. But freedom came with caveats: 'I was told if you talk about what happened you will be taken back to the concentration camp and never be let out. When I came home in 1939 to my parents and my family, I didn't tell them what happened in the concentration camp.' He spent four weeks with his family before leaving for the UK in May 1939. He would never see his father, mother or brother again.

He arrived in the UK with no English, one small suitcase and ten shillings and found work in the East End fitting sewing machines for making army uniforms.

In June 1940 he was arrested again – this time by British police. He was one of 2,000 German and Austrian Jewish internees herded onto the troopship Dunera. They weren't told where they were going and were kept 23 hours a day for nine weeks in foul and overcrowded conditions. 'Some people called it the floating concentration camp. I wouldn't go as far as that. We were below deck, no ventilation, no proper beds. There were a few hammocks that older people slept in – we slept on wooden tables. We had nothing. I read a book of someone who

Willy Field: born in Bonn in August 1920, died in Britain in May 2012

was on the Dunera as well. He described it as much worse than I did. He was right. But I cannot do that. It is not my nature – I always found something good in something bad.'

And that is the key to this quietly remarkable man. 'I've never forgotten what happened and I never will forget, but for me you have to go ahead.' His wife Judy smiles; she is used to his optimism, and capacity to forgive. 'He's just like that,' she says.

'Judy is right, I am just like that. People say to me: why are you like this? You should be a nasty person. But it's my nature. I can't change. I was always a happy boy. Up to 1933 I was very happy, I had a wonderful childhood. I was brought up within the Jewish religion, but we were a liberal family. I believe in Jewishness, I believe in God, but I do not practise.

What I do and always have since I was a little boy, is say something before I go to sleep – "Give us a good day tomorrow and thank you very much for the day" – and I've been doing that ever since I remember. Even during the war.'

Judy and Willy met in London after the war. She was also a refugee from Germany and her father died in Auschwitz. 'The first time we met I liked her very much, she was lovely looking, beautiful long hair. She didn't really like me because I talked about the football league.' But Judy relented. 'She was easy going and we got along fantastically.' They have been getting on fantastically for 61 years and have two sons, seven grandchildren and four great-grandchildren.

Willy, still a passionate football fan and a lifelong Arsenal supporter, goes to the matches with one of his sons and two grandsons. 'Arsène Wenger sent me a very nice letter congratulating me on being such a long-standing member and hoping that I carried on. I shall carry on as long as I can walk down. I walk everywhere.'

After the gruelling Dunera journey, Willy was dumped in an internment camp in Australia where, behind the

Willy Field serving in the British forces during the war

barbed wire, football was a major distraction. A year later the British, finally embarrassed by the scandalous treatment of the internees, offered them the chance to return to the UK and join the Pioneer Corps. Four thousand men enlisted, many of whom went into active combat.

As Helen Fry says: 'The risks were high: Germans caught behind enemy lines were tortured and executed as traitors. The general public don't realise their contribution. The nation should be grateful to these silent heroes.'

Had Willy told them where to stick their offer, nobody could have blamed him – why should he put his life on the line for the British after all he had endured at their hands? He says he was giving something back to the country which had saved his life; he was protecting democracy and doing his bit to resist Hitler.

Following two years training in the Pioneer Corps, Willy joined the Royal Armoured Corps as a tank driver, changing his name from Hirschfeld to Field in case he was captured by the Germans. Posted to the 8th King's Royal Irish Hussars, he drove a Cromwell tank and took part in the Normandy landings, arriving in France three days after D-day. He was involved in heavy combat and was wounded in Holland when his tank took a direct hit. The only survivor, he still feels the pain of losing his comrades. After he recovered he returned to frontline fighting, reaching Germany in 1945.

In the midst of war he hoped his family had survived. 'You always hope.' And how did he feel towards the Germans he encountered? 'I never had any hate.'

But it would be a mistake to see Willy's good nature as making him any kind of push-over. Far from it: 'When I went through the German villages everything looked terrible, but I was never sorry about that. I was thinking "You deserved it. It was your own fault." I've never felt sorry for the Germans, never mind whether they were good Germans or bad Germans.

'When I went to Berlin for the

On Kristallnacht in 1938, the Gestapo came for him. He was taken to Dachau, where he experienced the prelude to the full-scale slaughter that was to come first time it was completely destroyed. The Germans were picking up bricks to build houses. They told me silly stories – "Oh how bad we've got it here. The Russians did this to us" – but I told them I didn't feel sorry for them. Why should I? "You brought it all on yourself. You did it. You couldn't say Heil Hitler or get rid of the Jews quick enough in 1933. You deserve everything you got."'

It was a wonderful moment for Willy when he drove his tank past Churchill at the victory parade in Berlin. But soon after, he heard what had become of his family through the Red Cross. 'My father died in a camp in Cologne on his way to a concentration camp, but my mother was able to bury him in a Jewish cemetery in Cologne. That was a miracle. I only found that out twenty years ago.

'My mother, my brother, my uncle and my aunts were taken to the concentration camp in Minsk and died in 1941 or 42.' Only he and his twin sister Thea survived – she too had made it to the UK before the war.

For a long time Willy didn't talk to his sons about the past: 'They knew where I came from and what I did, but I never talked about the horrors of the concentration camp. It was difficult – you didn't want to talk about it.'

But in 1997 he started visiting a group of primary-school children in Bonn and told them his story. He went on visiting them every year and in 2001 he returned to Dachau for the first time, accompanied by the children he had got to know. Once again he stood on that parade ground, he saw the ledger with his name registering his arrival, he found the hut he had been confined to. It was overwhelming.

Willy still has a trace of his German accent but feels British and thinks and dreams in English, although he counts in German. England, he says, gave him his freedom. It gave him a life he has enjoyed, a marriage, two sons, a respectable career and much else.

I realised I was trying to elicit 'meaning of life' revelations from Willy. But it's not his style. His words are simple, direct and understated. Despite his experiences, his bravery, and his resilient spirit, he is modest, forgiving and straightforward. That is his wisdom. ◍

Willy Field's story can also be accessed through the AJR audio-visual Holocaust Testimony Archive: see www. refugeevoices.co.uk

De'Ath, You cur, Quit your wretched thrashing, it's ruining our reflections …

Kingsley, Martin and I
Wilfred De'Ath ponders the mixed Amis bag

I was born mid-way between the two famous Amises, Kingsley and Martin. Kingsley (born 1925) was 12 years older than me, Martin (born 1949) was 12 years younger.

I liked Kingsley because he wrote a first novel, *Lucky Jim*, which still makes me laugh out loud. (I re-read it once a year and always find something fresh in it.)

I like Martin because he wrote a brilliant first novel, *The Rachel Papers*, which says all there is to say about how to lose a girlfriend. (I don't re-read it so often, but I admire it.)

I disliked Kingsley because he sat between Auberon Waugh and myself at a *Private Eye* lunch some years ago and addressed himself exclusively to me, ignoring Bron. When I asked him why, he said it was because Bron had once had the temerity to criticise one of his books. This struck me as churlish.

I dislike Martin because he crudely propositioned my beautiful daughter when she turned up to interview him for a student magazine. The little shit! However, having just read his latest, *The Pregnant Widow*, borderline pornography, I would guess that my daughter was only one of many. Not that that lets him off the hook…

My acquaintance with Kingsley began in 1961 when I interviewed him for a radio documentary, *The Realm of Perhaps*, about science fiction, of which he had read a great deal and even written a book *New Maps of Hell*. We got on well and he kindly invited me to dine on the high table at Peterhouse, Cambridge, where he had just been appointed as English don. The food was superb – the main reason, so he confided in me, he had accepted a fellowship there. I couldn't help contrasting the handsome, slim man he was with the shuffling booby I sat next to at *Private Eye* twenty years later.

In the late 1960s, we both became temporary film critics, he for the *Observer*, I for the *Illustrated London News*. At the morning press shows, if the film was boring, which it usually was, Kingsley would slip out for a snifter, relying on me to brief him later over lunch. I didn't mind doing this because I enjoyed his company and was vain enough to think that he enjoyed mine (I didn't discover what he really thought about me until his Collected Letters appeared about ten years ago).

Before penning this, I took another glance at *Lucky Jim* and *The Rachel Papers*. There is no doubt that Kingsley was a very good novelist. There is no doubt either that Martin is – I say it through gritted teeth – very nearly a great one. What holds him back? How does he fall short? I can give the answer in a word based on my own bitter self-knowledge. Narcissism. ◍

Embrace riverside later living, at Riverstone Fulham

With sophisticated design and a range of outstanding amenities, Riverstone Fulham is offering an exceptional lifestyle on the River Thames exclusively for people over 65.

With 1, 2 and 3-bedroom apartments for sale, each with a private balcony or terrace – many of which have stunning river views – Riverstone Fulham has been created for you to be able to live in a vibrant community, whilst also having easy access to London's cultural attractions.

From tranquil morning walks along the river and effortlessly accessing Fulham's boutique shops and parks, to finding new friendships - you can make the most of the very best of Fulham living.

At Riverstone, we strongly believe in the power of community. It's central to our DNA, which is why we actively encourage all our residents to invite friends and family to enjoy the wealth of amenities available.

Why not catch up over a coffee at the Espresso Bar, practise your swing in the Golf Simulator, challenge new neighbours to a game of bridge in the Club Room, take a refreshing dip in the Pool, or simply relax in the Sauna... the choice is yours.

Grandchildren will love the Private Cinema, featuring cosy chairs, popcorn and an extensive library of films and blockbusters. Enjoy a meal with the family at Maria G's, our all-day

brasserie-style Restaurant & Bar, which is also open to the wider community and overlooks the River Thames.

New residents automatically join our members' community, The Riverstone Club. Alongside access to the outstanding amenities, The Riverstone Club offers a curated calendar of informal gatherings over shared interests, special guest speakers and exclusive events through our exciting partnerships with the Royal Albert Hall, Saatchi Gallery, Royal Philharmonic Orchestra, English National Opera and Glyndebourne Opera Festival and so much more.

With a proactive approach to health and wellbeing, we also work with residents to understand their priorities and offer wider health support through our selected expert partners and care through The Good Care Group, should you need it.

Retirement can mean many things to many different people. For us, it's all about 'rewriting the retirement rulebook' - doing things your way, supported by a vibrant and flexible living environment. Whether you want to stay living in the same area that has so much to offer, but are keen to "right size", wish to move closer to family – perhaps returning to London after residing in the countryside - or simply seek a place where you can lock up and leave, any time, safe in the knowledge that someone is looking after your home, we have all your needs covered.

What are you waiting for? Come and discover Riverstone Fulham today.

Book your viewing today. Take a tour of our stunning show apartments and amenities and meet the team. Email enquiries@riverstoneliving.com; call 020 3839 8557; or visit riverstoneliving.com.

Riverstone
FULHAM

Prices start from £860,000.*
Ts & Cs apply / *Other fees apply.
Prices correct at time of publication.

Dr Stuttaford's surgery

The power of honey

Your medical queries answered by our resident doctor

Tackling dry skin

A Scottish reader in her fifties has always suffered from dry skin. She is reconciled to the inevitable flaky, inflamed hands that follow hard graft in the garden or an icy east wind blowing in from the North Sea, but is now worried because her skin troubles seem to be becoming worse rather than better with increasing years. Would honey-based hand creams help?

Most doctors, although recognising the nutritional value of honey, have always tended to be dismissive of its therapeutic value as a skin balm. I was probably as cynical as the majority of my colleagues until I joined my family practice in Norfolk. The local obstetrician at the Norfolk and Norwich Hospital at that time didn't prescribe any application for torn and stitched women after their deliveries other than dressings that smothered the damaged parts in honey.

'Wounds treated with honey seemed to heal as well, if not better, than those treated with antibiotics'

Even after broad-spectrum antibiotics became available, this obstetrician's patients seemed to recover as well, if not better, than those who had been treated with antibiotics. The patients may have grumbled about the messiness of the honey but in retrospect they were grateful for their clean wounds. I was impressed, even if I tended to take the easy route and prescribe something from the chemist's shelves for my own patients.

A few years ago Professor Peter Molan of Waikato University, Auckland, offered evidence that honey collected from bees

that fed off pollen from New Zealand's indigenous Manuka trees had exceptional antibacterial and anti-inflammatory properties. Manuka honey creams, gels and soaps for people such as our reader are now available, and it is claimed that these not only improve many complexions but also help with cracked and itchy skins. And unlike the Norwich surgeon's rather

crude dressings of honey, they are not messy.

Every year I eat pots of Norfolk honey, but for some time I have also been a fan of Manuka honey. Now, as soon as the frosts start and my hands become chapped, I shall make a point of searching out some of the Manuka range of hand creams as a possible alternative to steroid creams and ointments.

★ Great Bores of Today ★ No.27

'...I missed Wednesday's episode of *The Archers* because I had an appointment at the evening surgery but you can always catch up with the Omnibus edition which is on Sunday mornings which is a godsend Helen has been pushing herself too hard and it's getting on Tony's nerves if you ask me there'll be something wrong with the baby and serve her right I mean without a partner it's going to be tough going for her either way to my mind it's never been the same since Phil died and they don't talk about farming any more...'
© *Fant and Dick*

Get a wife – or a dog

A recently widowed man whose wife died from a heart attack wonders if his current loneliness is likely to hasten his own end. He has read that bereavement is a risk to life as well as to health.

It is accepted by doctors that the likelihood of death in both men and women is increased by bereavement. (There may of course be reasons why both husband and wife have heart disease which are unrelated to any grief response: although the genetic causes of cardiovascular disease are highly significant, so too is lifestyle, and spouses share not only the same environment but the same habits, exercise patterns, food and vices.)

The general rule is that unmarried men die sooner. Single men are more likely to eat junk food, consume excess alcohol, smoke more, take less exercise and have a less well organised life. They are also more prone to loneliness.

Five years ago an American study of 3,000 men with an average age of 62 showed that men who were living alone had higher levels of C-reactive protein than their happily married contemporaries. (C-reactive protein is a marker for the level of the body's inflammatory processes, and inflammation is a potent factor in the clogging process in the blood vessels that leads to heart attacks and strokes.)

In this study, those who had been able to maintain close family links or friendships had appreciably less heart disease. Loneliness is also linked to high blood pressure, another factor in heart attacks and strokes.

It seems that a significant factor in keeping heart disease at bay is the availability of somebody in whom one can confide. A wife or partner is the obvious choice, but failing that a good social life helps. Dogs also have a part to play – they provide an undemanding, uncritical ear, and even the idlest old fogey has to get up and walk his dog.

A social life provides interaction with others and an exchange of ideas and confidences. Even better, it may also lead to a new romantic interest and better health outcomes. Once his initial bereavement symptoms have diminished our reader should waste no time in establishing or rebuilding social links.

Raymond Briggs: Notes from the sofa

Digital blues

Old Age is another country; we do things differently here. Or is it that Yoof does things differently there?

Sometimes I feel I am living in a foreign country – another world. Even the dear old *Radio Times*, for decades our cosy fireside companion, offers this advice in answer to some simpleton.

'It's most likely a problem with Flash. Go to the Adobe website and make sure you've got the latest version: get adobe.com/flashplayer. If you're still having difficulty, make sure you've got cookies enabled and perhaps update your browser, particularly if you're using Mozilla Firefox. You need version 4.'

'Cookies?' Let alone 'cookies enabled'? 'Browser'? 'Mozilla Firefox'? In the same piece they mention 'Samsung Blu-ray' and 'What about an Android app?' What indeed. It's good to know 'it runs on all Android phones and tablets' – 'Tablets'? I've got packets of those – blood pressure... cholesterol... pain... 'tablets running software versions 1.6 and above, but not Honeycomb tablets'.

What a shame. Those Honeycomb tablets sound rather nice. It features 'a news ticker' and 'video available to non-Flash enabled devices'. So that's a relief, but I must find out if my device is non-Flash enabled or not. Where is my device anyway? I'm sure I've seen it somewhere...

It says we're 'all waiting for Panasonic to fix the problem with a firmware upgrade'. Such a relief again. I was about to call Mr Holmes, our village electrician, but nowadays he's getting a bit too old to come out; rickety knees or something.

I must ask him about my non-Flash enabled device, he's just the man, and of course, get an update on the firmware upgrade. Not sure I've ever seen a firmware. Quite looking forward to it.

This edition gives us the long-awaited news that we can now get 'buttons' so that we can share 'a link on Delicious, Digg, Reddit and StumbleUpon.

This replaces the old Recommend Function.' That is really good news – for some time now I've been worried about my Recommend Function. StumbleUpon sounds good, too, having in the last half hour fallen over while walking the dog. There is further invaluable advice.

'Check you can receive a DVB-S2 signal.' (I must do that now, excuse me.) 'If you can, use these tuning parameters... Satellite: Astra 2D tp.50; Frequency: 10,847 MHz (vertical polarity).' I must check our aerial – it was on a vertical pole but it blew over about a month ago. 'Modulation: DVB-S2 QPSK; Symbol Rate: 23.0; FEC: 8/9.'

The tiresome cliché 'catch up' is used frequently. Perhaps they are trying to drop a hint to us oldies. But before I 'catch up' I must go and have a lie-down.

My brain aches.

Unwrecked England

Stanley Spencer at Sandham Memorial Chapel

Candida Lycett Green

A stone's throw from 'Downton Abbey' (a gigantic swank of a pile called Highclere, flaunting the limitless wealth of Victorian Carnarvons), Sandham Chapel serves as a welcome antithesis.

I came to it through the ghost of well remembered woods, which the valiant Swampy and his tree-climbing warriors failed to save from the bulldozers, and turned off into Burghclere. The long straggle of a village lies low under the great rounded hump of Beacon Hill in gorsey country, all neat, cosy brick-and-tiled cottages between oaks and yews.

Thin smoke rose from the odd garden bonfire. Set back a little from the street, beyond an apple orchard, you might easily miss the modest little chapel looking a bit like a stranded suburban tube station between its two Queen Anne-style almshouses.

Stanley Spencer referred to it as his 'holy box'. It was the culmination of his dream. Stanley had spent the entire First World War in the ranks, first as a medical orderly at the Beaufort War Hospital near Bristol, then with the 68th Field Ambulance unit in Macedonia, and finally on the front line with the 7th Battalion of Berkshires. His vivid memories haunted him long after the war had ended. When, in 1923, he went to stay with his friend Henry Lamb in Dorset, he talked of little else but his desire to paint an everlasting memorial to the ordinary soldier.

Lamb wrote, 'Stanley sits at a table all day evolving acres of Salonica and

Above: the chapel, Burghclere, Hants
Opposite page: *The Resurrection of the Soldiers* **(1928–29) by Spencer**

Bristol war compositions.' The two of them discussed the possibility of raising the money through public subscription, but at the crucial moment, as though God had organized it, the Behrends dropped by.

They became captivated by Stanley's evocations, particularly Mrs Behrend, whose brother, Lieutenant Henry Willoughby Sandham, had died as a result of the Macedonian campaign.

A decision was soon taken to build a chapel to his memory: a blank canvas for Stanley's paintings. 'What ho, Giotto!' was Stanley's reaction when he heard the news. Curmudgeonly as he was, he

did his best to persuade the Behrends to build the chapel near his home at Cookham for his own convenience.

They stuck to their guns and by 1927 the chapel, near their home at Burghclere, was finished.

Once inside, I was stunned to a reverent silence. I stood in the middle of what in effect is a plain double-height shoebox and was encompassed by wall-to-ceiling paintings depicting the everyday life of a soldier. After a minute, the extraordinary memorial came completely alive. The weariness and fear of the soldiers' faces was tangible and I got pulled right into each of the nineteen paintings by their mesmerising details and peculiar perspectives. The poignant is mixed with the mundane – from a convoy arriving with wounded soldiers, a dugout on the Salonika front or scraping frostbite off a soldiers' feet on a hospital bed, to the business of scrubbing floors, sorting kit bags and laundry, filling tea urns or making jam butties. The depiction of washing wounded patients is like a modern Piero della Francesca.

The whole eastern end of the chapel is covered floor to ceiling in a painting entitled *The Resurrection of the Soldiers*. Hundreds of white wooden crosses are strewn chaotically across a war-torn battle-ground of soldiers, dead mules and a collapsed wagon, stretching back into the far distance.

It took the sprightly Stanley (five foot two inches and six stone twelve ounces) nearly a year to complete. The pale art deco altar frontal before it, embroidered by Madeline Clifton, reads 'We are such stuff as dreams are made on'. It's a lump-in-the-throat sort of place. ◑

For information and visiting hours, telephone the Sandham Memorial Chapel (01635 278 394) or visit www.nationaltrust.org.uk

'After a minute the extraordinary memorial came alive, and I got pulled right into each of the paintings by their mesmerising detail and peculiar perspectives'

ILLUSTRATED BY PETER BAILEY

When he was a little boy, *Paul Bird* used to hang around the bombsites of West Ham with his mates. Their lives were changed when they were befriended by the theatre director Joan Littlewood...

Joan and her nutters

I was born in West Ham on 18th July 1958 and until the age of ten I lived on a small street called Salway Road. My house was an end-of-terrace property with a shop-like front, and came with an outside bog and inside tin bath. It was later demolished under the Slum Clearance Act, but it wasn't a slum, it was my home!

Just across the road stood the Theatre Royal Stratford East, and adjacent to this was a street called Angel Lane which ran from Stratford Broadway to just past the theatre stage door. Angel Lane was a typical market street with little shops on both sides, from cafés, pie and mash and fish and chip shops to clothes and hardware shops. Market stalls and barrows lined the street with traders shouting and yelling, selling their wares. You could buy anything – fruit and veg, fish, eggs, stockings, knickers, men's pants, dog food – you name it, you could get it.

Next to my house was a bombsite, and on the opposite side of the road was a smaller bombsite full of rubbish and weeds. These wastelands were our playgrounds. We would play and dig holes and tunnels in search of treasure. We would often find old coins and scrap metal and go home filthy dirty but rich. We did all the other stuff, like upsetting the neighbours with games of 'knock down Ginger', and hanging about on street corners in general. Like most kids we got bored easily. But all that changed when we came across Joan Littlewood and her Theatre Workshop.

We were hanging about on the corner of the smaller bombsite and out of what seemed nowhere, this strange woman, wearing a light blue merchant seaman's cap, approached us. She introduced herself as Joan and started asking questions. 'What's your name? How old are you? What are you doing? Why are you hanging about on street corners?' She had a very calming voice, and although very inquisitive, she had a kind manner about her, and seemed really interested in us.

She turned to her assistant, Christine. 'Can't we do something for these kids? Can't we get this place cleaned up, get them involved, and get them doing something?'

Christine nodded in agreement, and within weeks things did happen. We started to get the place cleaned up. Everyone got involved, including local residents. Joan got onto the council and we got planning permission to turn the site into a play area. We got a lot of help from local tradesmen and building companies. I think Christine would flutter her eyelashes and all sorts of things came our way for free – gloves, picks, shovels, paint, sand, cement and lots more. We even got builders to come over and lay slabs and put down flat concrete surfaces of all different colours giving us perfect play areas.

Come the cold winter night, things weren't so good, so Joan would let us into the theatre, but we had to stay quiet and behave ourselves. We would sit up in the gods and Joan would be up there too, scribbling notes on her clipboard. She did this without looking, her eyes and ears were fixed on the stage. We saw the shows so many times, we knew the lines and the words to the songs. I still remember some of the songs. (My favourite productions were *The Projector* and *Mrs Wilson's Diary*.) Not only that, we got to know the cast members too, and after rehearsals Joan would get the actors to do little sketches with us, getting us to improvise and have a bit of fun on stage.

After Joan's death, a special appreciation night was arranged at the National Film Theatre. As I took my seat I bumped into one of the actors who used to play-act with us, and not only did he recognise me, but he remembered my name. I couldn't believe it after forty years! He went on to recall how Joan would make him and his fellow actors

'Come the cold winter nights, Joan would let us into the theatre, but we had to stay quiet and behave ourselves. We would sit up in the gods and Joan would be up there too, scribbling notes on her clipboard'

act out these little sketches with us. It was an order. In fact, everyone working in the theatre – electricians, carpenters, wardrobe and scenery workers etc – was told to give up a little time to teach us things about their trades. I don't think they were happy about this – after all, they had a job to do, didn't they?

One day it was arranged for me and another kid called Paul Prendergast to meet the theatre's pianist. We were always bashing about on the piano and Joan thought we needed lessons, so this young musician was ordered to give them. We were taught the basics then shown exercises to practice in our spare time. The musician was called Carl Davis. Today he is a conductor with the London Philharmonic Orchestra and a composer who has written music for hundreds of television programmes and films.

Joan always had time for us, and she was very generous. We used to visit her office most days to say hello and have a chat. It was a small room at the top of the theatre, just outside the upper circle, and had a low ceiling which you could reach up and touch. Joan would be there working away and smoking French cigarettes, but she would always break off to talk. We were standing there talking one day, and all of a sudden Joan shouted, 'Look at your shoes. You can't walk around like that.' We looked down

at the kid standing next to me and his toes were poking out. Joan shook her head and gave him two pounds and said 'For Christ's sake, go and get some new shoes.'

Even when she was under pressure or stressed she'd still have time for us. Well, almost. Once, we went up to see her, and she was really stressed – she was probably working on her next production or trying to work out how to pay the theatre's electric bill or the actors' wages. Then, in a very kind way, she told us to 'Sod off and play somewhere else'.

But having said that, she then smiled at us, gave us five bob and told us to get an ice cream.

One Sunday she decided to take us all to lunch.

'We're going to China Town, to my favourite restaurant.'

'What food we having?'

'Chinese,' she replied.

'OK, thanks, that sounds nice.'

But then we thought, China Town? Blimey, the furthest we'd ever been was to Canning Town!

China seemed a long way to go, and what was Chinese food? We soon found out, and about twenty of us piled into this restaurant in Limehouse. None of us had ever been to a restaurant, and none us had ever sampled foreign food. We loved every minute of our exotic experience and, yet again, Joan picked up the tab.

Joan had a pet name for us – she called us her 'nutters'. I can't work out why, but she did. It would be my nutters this, my nutters that, and so on. It wasn't to offend, it was a term of endearment. Even years later, she would write letters to me and refer to her 'nutters' and how she missed them. She went on to tell me how talented, bright and alive we were and that she'd back our gang against Eton! That's not bullshit, she meant it.

In 1968 my house in Salway Road was demolished, just like everything else around it. Only the theatre was saved, thank God! I moved to a new house only about half a mile away and shortly after I moved from primary school to senior school. Because of other distractions I sort of lost contact with the theatre and Joan. She carried on until Gerry Raffles's death in 1975 and then I believe she went to live in France.

I never forgot those wonderful times. One evening in 1994 I watched Omnibus on BBC television, and there she was, in my front room. What a shock. All those years and she was still around. I had to make contact. I wrote a letter to her and sent it to the BBC to pass on. She received it and we kept in contact by letter for years. I also arranged a reunion and got hold of a few nutters from the past. We made a date to meet at one of Joan's favourite restaurants in Great Windmill Street. We all arrived together including Christine. Joan loved it. It was a complete surprise – Christine had managed to get her down to Soho for the night and the nutters were there. She couldn't believe it.

Joan Littlewood by Jane Bown

Joan died on the 20th September 2002, just two weeks after my own father had died. I was really down after hearing of Joan's death but that all changed when I was invited, along with other nutters, to attend her funeral.

It was probably the best funeral that I'd ever been to. Joan's order of the day was quite simple, No priests, no vicars, no hymns, no religion – just fun and laughter. And we certainly got it.

I've managed to recall only a few of my memories from those days, but there were many more. If only the other kids were here with me now, as I write – between us, we could write a book. I will never forget Joan and what she brought to us: the arts, culture and my love for the theatre.

Joan Littlewood, 1914-2002, RIP. ◑

'Let's talk about this, Hilary! There must be another way to meet the council tax demand'

'Do you think they'll ever rise up and try to overthrow us?'

'Mum, lovely to see you, come in'

Safer bathing from the mobility experts

NOW WITH A 15 YEAR WARRANTY*

Slip-resistant surfaces

Integrated riser grab bar

Stylish folding seat

"My husband and I would like to thank you for the superb makeover. We are delighted with your service"
Mr & Mrs R Pleasants

At Premier Care, our extensive range of stylish **easy-access showers** and **walk-in baths** have been designed to give people with increasing mobility issues the confidence to bathe safely and securely in style and comfort.

Our all-inclusive service means we take care of everything, from design through to expert installation by one of our skilled teams. We even clean up after ourselves. All you need do is enjoy your new bathroom.

- A complete service that will transform your bathroom and your life.

- Peace of mind - helping tens of thousands of people for over 30 years.

Premier Care in Bathing - the UK's No.1 for stylish wet rooms, easy access showers and walk-in baths.

For your FREE brochure call us today:

0800 988 4232

Ref PCM401

* Call 0800 988 4232 for more details

BRITISH INSTITUTE OF KBB INSTALLATION
PARTNER

COVID-19 AWARE

HAND SANITISER
SOCIAL DISTANCING
PPE

Premier Care™
in Bathing

www.premiercareinbathing.co.uk

Good morning, campers!

Cheap and cheerful, with a dash of Southern European atmosphere, Butlin's continues to pull in the families. It's just a pity they've dropped the knobbly knees contests, says *Zenga Longmore*

ILLUSTRATED BY MARTIN HONEYSETT

Butlin's is the only holiday my children and grandchildren consider to be a treat – no other place will do, and we've been to Butlin's for the last ten years. Yes, I'm well aware everyone sneers at Butlin's and praises holidays sur Le Continon but – if they only knew – Butlin's is (in one way at least) surprisingly similar to Southern Europe. In Italy you'll see grannies, parents and bambini publicly eating and drinking noisily together far into the night. Butlin's must be the only place this side of the Channel where you'll witness the same spectacle. In the evening, grown-ups and children dance crazily together to music provided by a chubby Lady Gaga impersonator. Babies

lie asleep in prams, impervious to the racket. Even the teenagers can have fun as they craftily knock back alcopops while looking fashionably contemptuous.

This year our exuberant party consisted of my dear friend Jennifer and a lot of offspring, some mine, some hers and some other people's, aged from five to sixteen. We chose the Minehead holiday camp. It's cheap, it's loud and the Redcoats provide a comforting, old fashioned quality. If it rains it doesn't matter – there is Splash Waterworld for the brave-hearted and Bob the Builder indoor rides for the timid. If you're very bored, and it rains for several days, there are endless shows featuring a sinister purple dinosaur.

I was, however, extremely disappointed to see how sophisticated the nightlife had become. Butlin's used to uphold the finest traditions of vulgar music hall, with Northern comics organising jolly singalongs. Knobbly knees competitions are now but a golden memory. A beefy Asian Michael Jackson delighted the disco throng with his moonwalking, but he lacked the jaunty gravitas of 'Ten Ton' Arkwright, who, if I remember rightly, used to host the Biggest Beer Belly competitions up in Skeggy.

Speaking of disappointment, does anyone know why the Butlin's' cuisine now resembles pre-Jamie Oliver school dinners? As we entered the food hall,

In Italy you'll see grannies, parents and bambini publicly eating and drinking noisily together far into the night. Butlin's must be the only place this side of the Channel where you'll witness the same spectacle…

our nostrils were assaulted by a 1970s school-dinnery stench. But we had paid for the 'All You Can Eat' buffet and were determined to get our money's worth. The Traditional Fayre advertised as 'roast beef and Yorkshire pudding' turned out to be processed sandwich meat, greyish broccoli and rock-hard sawdusty pellets which my daughter assured me were stuffing balls, although I think they were badly disguised Yorkshire puddings. As soon as it became submerged by the gooey gravy, the 'roast beef' disintegrated into slime, like a snail taking a warm salt bath.

Not that anyone cared. Most of the diners at the 'Eat All You Can' just wanted to eat all they could, without being too fussed as to what it was. As an experienced Butliner I should be used to the size of my fellow campers by now, but every year I find my alarm increases at the same rate as their waistlines. Darwin believed our species evolved from blobs into humans. A glance at the Butliners of Minehead would have convinced him that he had got it the wrong way round. Everyone looked as if they were wearing giant rubber swimming pools. I had hoped the 'swimming-pool look' would never leave America, where it first became fashionable during the 1980s, but my hopes have been painfully dashed. Anyone who holds with clever theories explaining why we have grown so grotesquely overweight (toxins from plastics, food additives, etc) should visit Butlin's, where it is apparent that the sole reason so many

people are so fat is that they simply never stop eating.

Few Butliners can be spotted without something edible in their hands and mouths. From the dinner hall they'll waddle to the doughnut stand from which they'll lumber to the burger bar, finally coming to rest at the ice-cream counter before rolling off again to the doughnuts. It was not too unpleasant a sight for me as it was a novelty to feel painfully thin.

On our last day I decided to take everyone to Dunster Castle. Set atop a wooded hill, it resembles an enchanted fortress out of an Arthur Rackham fairy story. During the Civil War it served as the prison of William Prynne, a mad Puritan author of endless tracts denouncing theatre. 'Stage playes are of the Deville, therefore they needes must be eville,' he wrote. Charles I, whose wife was something of a thespian, was so unimpressed by Prynne's sentiments that he had Prynee 'eared' for his pains.

When I suggested leaving Butlin's for the day to go to a 'pointless castle,' I feared I too was about to be eared – or worse – by the children. There were 'sik' funfair rides they were going to miss ('sik' being the latest kiddy slang for 'wonderful'). Why was I taking them to the countryside? 'A castle? You're clapped! You're never happy till you've, like, so ruined our holiday. Why do you always have to come with us? Year after year?' shrieked my friend's twelve-year-old daughter (rather rudely, I thought). But no child, however impolite, is impervious to bribery, so after many false promises of trainers, iPods and the like, I succeeded in steering everyone to the mediaeval village of Dunster.

Once in Dunster Gardens the children joyously climbed trees and spent three screaming hours rolling down flowery hills. Even the ill-mannered twelve-year-old had fun jumping out at elderly tourists in her guise of the cackling ghost of William Prynne. As we ladled clotted cream onto warm scones in the Dunster tea room, funfairs and amusement arcades faded into a silver mist.

Here I am, back in my Harlesden home. For four days, thanks to the Butlin's' beef, my diet has consisted of natural yogurt, peppermint tea and charcoal tablets. I don't think my digestive system will ever fully recover. The twelve-year-old and her sisters are demanding we go to the Bognor Butlin's next year. They've been to the Ivory Coast, Spain and Jamaica. Last year they stayed in a dacha in a remote corner of Russia. But nowhere in the world, they say, can beat Butlin's. 'Butlin's,' so they tell me, 'is sik' (sic). ◍

Pearls of Wisdom

Colin Thubron

The eminent travel writer and novelist talks to
Melanie McFadyean

Colin Thubron CBE is one of our greatest writers, with many awards and twenty-one books to his name, most of them travel writing but also seven novels. 'My travel books spring from curiosity about worlds which my generation has found threatening: China, Russia, Islam – perhaps from a desire to humanise and understand them,' he has written. 'The novels seem to be reactions against this, and mostly arise from more introverted, personal concerns, often being set in enclosed places.' After Eton he went into publishing and, briefly, TV. For his latest book, *To a Mountain in Tibet*, he climbed to 18,600 feet, following the pilgrims' trail around Mount Kailas in the Himalayas. Aged 73, he is married and lives in London.

Your curiosity seems undimmed by age.
I suppose it's a kind of optimism – the feeling that there will always be something interesting and fascinating round the corner. I don't go into a country with a sense of understanding, however heavy my research has been. So the books, I hope, transmit expectations from an author who is taking the reader through a journey of discovery – including its innocence, mistakes, misapprehensions and understandings. So perhaps that is why the vitality appears to remain.

Do the journeys get easier?
I may know a bit more about how to travel wisely, but I don't feel any more in command of my subject when I start out. I don't feel fear before a journey, just excitement and curiosity and an odd sense of invulnerability – but of course there are always anxieties before leaving about what's going to happen, and especially about whom you are going to meet. My books are predicated

on people. A journey is dead unless you experience the culture – and that is mostly experienced through the people I meet.

I am appalled looking back to my earliest books, on Damascus for example, because I couldn't speak Arabic. I now have the basis of Russian and Mandarin, and awful tourist Arabic. Mandarin and Russian take you through a great deal of Asia – most of central Asia has a lingua franca of Russian. There is great delight in an interesting conversation with someone who lives in the land in which you are travelling. People's lives are always extraordinary.

What do you take with you?

As little as possible. Before leaving, I lay out everything I think I need, then ask myself do I really need that? The answer is almost always no. But I always take a compass: my sense of direction is very strong – but usually wrong.

Do you feel wiser with age?

I suppose I feel I'm an old fool really. I feel less and less certain about anything. There's a quote I love from Newton, towards the end of his life: 'I do not know what I may appear to the world, but to myself I seem to have been only like a boy playing on the seashore, and diverting myself in now and then finding a smoother pebble or a prettier shell than ordinary, whilst the great ocean of truth lay all undiscovered before me.'

What is troubling about ageing?

You have less time, and time becomes more precious. The proportion between what's possible and what you apprehend to be out there somewhere is more and more weighted against your ever discovering anything much, so it becomes more important to travel, to discover, to read, because while there's less time, the burden of what has to be understood is greater. You feel you could have led numberless other lives.

In Among the Russians you say you have 'a restless inner life and a distrust of belonging'. Why the distrust of belonging?

Probably I meant distrust of belonging to anywhere specific, to anyone specific. That would have grounded me, and at that age I wouldn't have wanted to be grounded. Belonging meant a narrowing down of possibility.

Mount Kailas, Tibet

Was it some early experience that made you feel that way?

Did you think the death of my sister made me distrust loving? I don't think so. But in my teens I was quite Christian. I wished to hold onto that, and even after my sister's death – I was only 19 when she died – I wanted to believe in an afterlife.

Coincidentally I started my first job as an apprentice in a publishing firm the week she died, and there were all these books. I became ravenously fascinated by everything and alert and alive in ways I hadn't been before. My teenage Christianity seemed too constrictive. I had built it up as a delicate edifice and then one day the whole thing crashed to bits. It was a tremendous relief, really, because in a sense I'd been excusing Christianity, its concepts of the afterlife and hell and so on.

When you wrote *To a Mountain in Tibet*, your mother had died, leaving you the last of your family. Did you find an accommodation with death?

My journey's motive was more visceral than intellectual but I realize that I was testing the idea of what we think of as an individual. In Hindu Buddhism there is no personal survival, no soul, no God. What survives is the weight of good or evil in the world, that gets carried on as karma, which has no individual property. It put one's own life in perspective – one's self isn't so important. On this sort of journey you're walking the earth, it's a pilgrimage in a sense. It could have made a lovely narrative if it had ended in enlightenment or catharsis, but it didn't. In some way it reconciled me to the idea of my own death. Yet I don't close the gates to anything, because I think life is entirely incomprehensible and mysterious. I really don't understand a thing. There's that old story of the Viking feast. A bird flies in from the dark across the hall and goes out the other end through an open door into darkness again. That's a synonym for human existence – a creature comes in out of total darkness and disappears into darkness. Why we happen to be here now seems infinitely curious.

Do you get lonely on those journeys?

Loneliness is incomprehensible to me. I love solitude. But I got married a year ago for the first time and now I would probably feel lonely without my wife.

Do you regret having had no children?

Not achingly. You fantasise about an ideal daughter but when I look at other people's children I'm not greatly encouraged. I don't know how good a father I'd have been. Solitude is essential to the sort of work I do.

Are you fit enough in your seventies to go on with these arduous journeys? Don't you feel more afraid?

Nobody is as well as they wish to be at my age. But one's mental state is far more important than one's physical ☞

state. You can go on doing stuff if you wish it and you're curious enough. I'm naturally fairly fit. I like tennis but I don't play as much as I should. I've got a bad knee but have had that since I was seven. It hurts a bit on the tennis court and going downhill.

Have you had any accidents?

I had a car crash in 1978. I'd like to say it was in Uzbekistan, but it was in East Grinstead. I had a broken back and shoulder. I was lucky not to be paralysed. I was on my back for weeks, but immobility has always been rather good for me because my mind goes wandering and concocts things. I concocted the idea that I wanted to walk along the Great Wall of China.

Have you got another big journey planned?

The next journey? I don't know. I don't like having to decide on one. I like it to insist on itself out of nowhere. I'm writing a novel at the moment. It's big and complicated, which may be a product of age, as it's much more contemplative than my previous ones.

There's melancholy running through your books as well as comedy.

Most people notice the melancholy, not the humour.

You don't seem like a melancholic fellow...

I'm not melancholic day to day. There's too much to be fascinated by, to enjoy – but there is an underlying melancholy, which is logical. As the Buddhist says, from all that he loves, man must part.

At what age are we old?

Old age is whatever's older than you by five years. I've been shocked into realising my age a few times. On the tube occasionally I am offered a seat, usually by a young woman. I think there must be someone behind me with grey hair, or hair even whiter than mine. My instinct is to say no thank you, but it would be more gracious to accept. The idea of a freedom pass is grotesque, but I've accepted the grotesque because it makes life easier and I'm grateful for it.

How would you complete the phrase 'life is...'?

... idiotically short. ◉

Genius crossword 295
BY ANTICO (MAY 2013)

Clues are given according to alphabetical order of their answers, which should be entered jigsaw-fashion in the grid. The middle column is occupied by the name of a product whose 9 (unclued) was born 150 years ago this month. 19 38 and 29 30 (all unclued) were also developed by the 9, whose first name was 10 (clued) and whose surname occupies the top row. Essential features of 29 30 occupy the bottom row.

Clues

Affair Oscar in funny article raised (5)
Notice tin with collar round (5)
Attack sailor in trouble at sea, losing time (8)
Woman gambles with yen (5)
Recipient of loan from bank restricted by drill? (8)
Scale in chapter with extension (5)
Records debate without us (5)
Be furious about missing fine bird (3)
Amount of work necessary to cover ground (3)
Open loud station (5)
Insect in endless dance rising (4)
Hard time for Olympian (4)
Man keeping old garden tool (3)
Material possessed by sheikh, a king (5)
Right after nap, wanting soft drink (3)
One detained by fat landowner (5)
Leather? Not available, old man (4)
Amphibian went swimming (4)
Part of job eliminating daggers (5)
Ring around tuberous plant (3)

Discordant aristocrat abandoned by leader on island (3-3)
Safe from hesitation, following favourite (5)
Capably arranged conclusion of work making sound reproduction (8)
Describes wine and beams (8)
Rebuke about opening of secret file (4)
Party mostly for rabbi (3)
Abolition disregarding a revolt (5)
Piece of music from new donor (5)
Garment turning up in fair assortment (4)
Runs projection, covered by press wrongly (8)
Main view in speech (3)
Very capricious being in revolutionary crowd with energy (8)
Chaos for all to see with supporters in retreat (5)
Dreadful din we increase (5)
Inclination to go north on vessel in place in Bedfordshire (6)
Period play's ending with attention (4)

Answers on page 123

Confused about Self Publishing?

Many unscrupulous companies will try to flatter you with lavish claims about how wonderful your book is and how it will just fly of the shelves!

Print 5000 copies. They will sell like hotcakes!

Publishing your own book can be a bit of a nightmare. There are all sorts of pitfalls for the unwary.

It costs HOW much?!

At **York Publishing Services** we don't do flattery. Or fibs. But we do know that we can make your book look fabulous. You won't need to re-mortgage or cash in your pension!
We are very proud to have been called "*a dolphin in a sea of sharks*" by one of our authors!

There are many companies just out to rip you off and take your money.
At YPS we don't expect you to pay for anything before we produce your books!

Most companies will try to fit your book into one of their 'packages'.
At YPS we don't have 'packages' and 'package prices'.
We think every author and every book is unique.
We think you should only pay for those services that you really need.

Copyediting & proofreading
Full book design service
Printing & binding
Promotion & marketing
Book distribution
Commission-free online bookshop
eBook production & distribution

yps york publishing services
Books from design to distribution

THE No1 BESTSELLER
Writers' & Artists' YEARBOOK 2014

YPS are recommended by the Writers' & Artists' Yearbook

writersandartists.co.uk

York Publishing Services Ltd
01904 431213
enquiries@yps-publishing.co.uk
www.yps-publishing.co.uk

At YPS we believe that advice should always be FREE. And that every book should start with a conversation or a cup of tea and a chat!

Beth Chatto

Designer, plantswoman and author Beth Chatto, 90 in June, is one of Britain's most influential gardeners. *David Wheeler* celebrates her career

Britain excels in raising influential amateurs – a band of knowing, achieving and sometimes revolutionary individuals who, in all but a few fields, can leave many a trained academic on the starting blocks.

When Beth Chatto hits ninety towards the end of June the horticultural world will be reminded of the profound garden-changing influences pioneered by one of Britain's greatest proponents – still active, though now at half speed.

Looking for someone of Beth's vintage who might have early recollections I called on Ronald Blythe, who notched up his own ninetieth birthday last November. 'One day in the early 1960s,' he tells me, 'whilst visiting the artist John Nash, he said, "What do you think? Beth Chatto is going to make a garden at Elmstead Market and wants us to take a look at the site." So he and I drove to a track which was very like that to his garden at Wormingford, although

on the level. And there was a gravel pit – nothing else. She and I were old friends – or, rather, young friends – and I never doubted her abilities to do anything... Her guru – and mine – was the plantsman-artist Sir Cedric Morris, whose garden at Benton End, Hadleigh, was where we often met.'

My own adventures with Mrs Chatto began some twenty years later with possession of my first proper garden – a third of an acre on the Surrey/Hampshire border where the soil was little more than desert sand. It coincided with a book that Beth might have written specially for me: The Dry Garden. A few years later, living in mid Wales, where annual rainfall was quadrupled, I turned to its companion, The Damp Garden. A steady flow of inspired and inspiring books has followed ever since and these, plus visits to Beth's Essex nursery and garden, have taught me much of what I know and, more importantly, what I understand, about plants and gardens.

Another habitué at Benton End was

CLOCKWISE FROM LEFT: the Scree Garden, which includes five island beds, provides a home for many small plants that would be out of scale in the main Gravel Garden; Beth Chatto; the Water Garden.

the young Elizabeth David (with whom I had a friendship during the last ten years of her life) and although the two women hadn't met for many years, Beth renewed their acquaintance in the 1970s while in London exhibiting at a Chelsea Flower Show where, it almost goes without saying, she scooped up top prizes for a decade or more. This renewal of friendship resulted in me driving the frail E.D. (she was born in 1913) to Beth's White Barn House on a blowy spring day when an east wind left Elizabeth tense with cold, but which the hardy B.C. considered no more than a balmy southern breeze.

In a long and dedicated life Beth has lectured in many parts of the world, making chums as easily as a willow makes roots. Her friendship with the late Christopher Lloyd was immortalised in Dear Friend and Gardener, a 1998 volume of plant-and-people chatty letters to and from each other. And that Sussex connection continues with Lloyd's 'right-hand man', Fergus Garrett, who describes Beth as one of life's 'great givers', likening her attitude to plants and people to a 'religious experience'.

Steven Wooster has photographed Beth's garden over many years. 'She was always supportive, and would let me know if I hadn't quite captured her vision, and that honest feedback was something I greatly appreciated.'

In 1987 Beth Chatto received the Royal Horticultural Society's highest award, the RHS Victoria Medal of Honour, a precursor to her appointment as OBE in 2002.

I still take every opportunity to see Beth's diverse acres. As Ronald Blythe blithely says, 'She made a unique garden – and a celebrated one.'

Many happy returns, Beth. ◖

• *The Beth Chatto Gardens, Elmstead Market, Colchester CO7 7DB Telephone 01206 822 007. For more information visit the website at www.bethchatto.co.uk Beth Chatto: 27th June 1923-13 May 2018*

The Gravel Garden in high summer

A steady flow of Beth's inspiring books, plus visits to her nursery and garden, have taught me much of what I know and, more importantly, what I understand, about plants and gardens

Larry's crew

When the National Theatre celebrated its fiftieth anniversary, theatre critic *Peter Lewis* recalled the early days under its inaugural artistic director, Laurence Olivier

When the National Theatre opened its doors on October 22nd, fifty years ago, it was on a Hamlet that everyone preferred to forget. Laurence Olivier said it was about the worst Hamlet that he could remember – and he had directed it. The setting was cumbersome. The revolve failed and had to be pushed round by hand. And the lead performance was 'telephoned in' by Peter O'Toole from somewhere distant – possibly Arabia where he had just enjoyed an international triumph as T E Lawrence. The one thing that had worked was the theatre itself, the legendary Old Vic. Succeeding directors of the National have spent forty of its fifty years trying to humanise the concrete stack that replaced it on the South Bank. There was no need to humanise the Old Vic, battered, rather shabby, but warm and welcoming and tasting of past glories.

There was little money for refurbishment, or staff, or actors' salaries, which began at £14 a week plus £1 per performance. The director himself drew little over £100 a week. There was no space for offices. The National was administered from some wooden contractors' huts in an alleyway of nettles and brambles grandly called Aquinas Street. If you could find it, you addressed yourself to a window marked Enquiries. The atmosphere was reminiscent of wartime – a small RAF station, perhaps, where productions were rehearsed and launched like fighter planes, some of which were doomed to crash. The Wing Commander, Olivier, wore a uniform of pinstripes and boardroom spectacles. He was well suited to be the last actor-manager, the guv'nor, known to all as 'Sir'. He cared for his troupe and was with them day and night, lunching with them in the canteen on an apple, piece of cheese and glass of champagne, sometimes sitting with the stage hands.

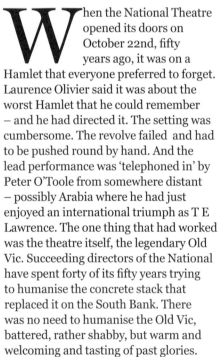

Olivier aimed to create a small company, his, not the nation's, capable of playing anything. Asked what was his policy he replied, 'To make the audience applaud'. Applause was his life's blood. The company he had recruited was dazzlingly young. Instead of his old associates (and rivals) he chose actors at the start of their careers and he picked well: Finney, Stephens, Jacobi, Hopkins, McKellen, Finlay, Gambon, to skim merely the cream, and among the women Geraldine McEwan and Joan Plowright, by then his wife. Maggie Smith gave up West End stardom and her percentage of the box office to join them. They were eager to learn from a master of their craft.

It was Kenneth Tynan, his literary manager, who persuaded Olivier to do the one Shakespeare role he had always resisted – Othello. It was a virtuoso exhibition of

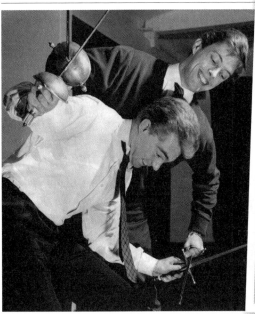

Facing page, clockwise from left: the Old Vic; Laurence Olivier with a Variety Club award for his performance in Othello; Peter O'Toole during the opening night of Hamlet, the National's inaugural production, 22nd October 1963
This page, clockwise from left: Derek Jacobi (left) and William Hobbs rehearsing the duel scene for the National Theatre production of *Hamlet*; Geraldine McEwan; Maggie Smith as Desdemona and Laurence Olivier as *Othello*, 1965; Joan Plowright with friends in the Old Vic foyer, 23rd October 1963

blacking up, not only in appearance but in behaviour – the hip-swaying gait, eyeball-rolling deep bass delivery of the lines rising to a keening treble on 'The pity of it, Iago!' The pity of it failed to move some experienced members of the audience. 'Larry doesn't do agony,' said Sybil Thorndike. But it packed the theatre and had to be much repeated, exhaustingly for him.

Olivier led his company a very long way. There were four marvellous years which included Redgrave's *Uncle Vanya* and Zeffirelli's Sicilian *Much Ado*, as well as new home-bred plays

like Peter Shaffer's *Royal Hunt of the Sun* and Tom Stoppard's *Rosencrantz and Guildenstern are Dead*. But he wore out his health in the effort, and his withdrawal for cancer treatment led to a couple of seasons so disappointing that I remember writing of the National as 'panned, pampered and half empty'. Not for the first time he had to act his company back out of the red. His Shylock was followed by possibly his finest performance in O'Neill's study of his own misery-making family, *A Long Day's Journey Into Night*. The play runs four hours yet seemed quite short. It was a

night of theatre history that I would hate to have missed.

While he was playing James Tyrone so hypnotically, the NT Board was arranging for him to be replaced by Peter Hall as director to move the company into the new building when – if ever – it was ready. When he discovered the deal that had been fixed behind his back Olivier let out a howl of pain: 'They've given me the boot – again!' His fury (he did not want Hall as his successor) made the transition an unhappy one. He refused to set foot on the new stage named after him except once, to welcome the Queen. ◑

The atmosphere was reminiscent of wartime – a small RAF station, perhaps, where productions were launched like fighter planes, some of which were doomed to crash

Paul Bailey remembers his great friend,
the cookery writer Jane Grigson

My kitchen goddess

I met Jane Grigson in the summer of 1975, as the result of a review I wrote of her husband Geoffrey's book *Britain Observed* in the New Statesman. Geoffrey was, and remains, one of my literary heroes, not least for his fiercely independent spirit and his talent for expressing considered opinions that went against the fashionable grain. It would become apparent in the years to come that Jane loved him for those very same qualities. He said things, she confided in me once, she would never dare to say, however much she wanted to.

Jane was Geoffrey's third, and last, wife. He was her senior by almost 23 years, but the age difference didn't matter to her. In her late twenties she had fallen for the art critic and curator Bryan Robertson, with whom she worked in a London gallery, but she soon realised it was a hopeless infatuation when she discovered he was gay. (In the last year of her life I reunited Jane and Bryan at a lunch I prepared for them. It was a joyous occasion, enlivened by gossip and laughter. I have seldom been such a happy listener.) Bryan had hoped that Jane would find her ideal older man one day, and so it was to be. Jane, who had admired Geoffrey's work – his study of Samuel Palmer and his Shell guides to birds and flowers, especially – when she was a schoolgirl, thought she was the luckiest woman in the world after meeting him and learning that her feelings for him were reciprocated.

The Grigson family was in something close to disarray when Jane and Geoffrey married. If anyone knew how to soothe the famous curmudgeon's savage breast, it was the bright young woman from Sunderland. She moved into the house he owned at Broad Town in Wiltshire and transformed it into a loving place. It seemed that she would be content for ever with her early married life, as she typed and corrected Geoffrey's manuscripts. Everything was to change in the 1960s when one of their neighbours in Trôo, in Loir-et-Cher, in

Jane Grigson and her daughter Sophie

France, asked Jane to be his secretary and researcher. Adey Horton was late delivering a book on *Charcuterie and French Pork Cookery* for a London publisher. His agreed delivery date was already history when Jane agreed to come to his assistance. Horton was so impressed with her skills that he eventually handed the entire project over to her.

And that is how her career as a food writer began – accidentally. If Horton had been more diligent, Jane would have merited nothing grander than finding her name in the book's acknowledgements rather than on the front cover.

That first of her scholarly and approachable books was reviewed glowingly by Elizabeth David in the *Sunday Times* and achieved the rare distinction of being translated into French. It has become the standard work on the subject. *Good Things*, which came out in 1971, is my own favourite, not least because of the recipe for the wonderful curried parsnip soup she invented. For my mother's 87th birthday I cooked Honeycomb Mould, the pudding she rescued from the Victorian nursery. It is made with the juice and rind of lemons, with eggs, gelatine, sugar, cream and Guernsey milk. It has a cap of lemon jelly and beneath that a band of opaque cream jelly, and a honeycombed spongy base. My mother, who had worked in service from the age of thirteen, remembered the cook preparing it for the children in the grand house in Hampshire where she was first employed. That was before

the First World War. She had not seen or eaten it since then.

Jane was touched by this story. She liked it when food had a human and historical significance in people's lives. Her books and weekly articles for the *Observer* brought in the kind of money that Geoffrey, who had scraped together a living as a reviewer and anthologist for decades, had never dreamed of earning. He basked in her success. The meals I had with the two of them in Geoffrey's beautifully designed garden at Broad Town are among my happiest memories.

After Geoffrey's death in November 1985, Jane lost some of her sparkle, though she put on a show of cheerfulness in public. She still used the word 'daft', which she pronounced with a flat Geordie 'A', whenever she found something to laugh at. In the spring of 1989, I went with her on an eating tour of Scotland, to the Highlands and Lowlands. These were days of unalloyed pleasure, as we met chefs and restaurateurs and growers. I remember a picnic we shared at Loch Ness. The monster was in absentia, but there was a seabird that gobbled bread, cheese and salami as it perched on the bonnet of the car. 'Geoffrey would have identified it immediately,' she said. She opened a bottle of non-alcoholic wine someone had given her and poured us a glass each. After a couple of sips, she remarked 'It's disgusting, isn't it? Let's have the real thing.' So we did.

Jane died on 12th March 1990, the eve of her 62nd birthday, She had been anticipating death from cervical cancer for at least two years. In those final months, her chosen expression was 'Sod it all', with or without an accompanying laugh. Waking from a coma, she saw her beloved sister Mary weeping at her bedside. 'Oh, you silly cow' were her last words.

She was my best and dearest friend for a precious time. I think of her every day. How could I not? Her generous heart and soul are there in my kitchen, permanent tenants. *Ⓞ*

Pursuits

GARDENING
DAVID WHEELER
ROSES

By joining the Historic Roses Group (HRG) I have been admitted to a rarefied world of intoxicating colour and fragrance. While roses have been part of my gardening life since my teenage years, it is only now, in what should be my retirement years, that a lifelong interest in them has pretty much matured into an all-absorbing passion.

In recent months I have revelled in roses in southern Italy, Madeira, the Balearics and Morocco, places where they bloom up to eight weeks earlier than their British cousins, oozing scent that mingles in those warmer gardens with the potent whiff of citrus flowers and jasmine.

Gallicas, Portlands, Bourbons, Noisettes, Damasks, Chinas, Centifolias, Albas, Rugosas... they're enough to set my blood racing, while individual varietal names increase my heartbeat dangerously, with backstories as intriguing as their provenance. Who were Mrs Aaron Ward (bred in 1922), Mme Edouard Herriot (1913), Lady Sylvia (1926), Jules Margottin (1853), and who was the French quack whose name lives on in the mysteriously dark-hued 'Souvenir du Docteur Jamain' (1865)? The answers lie in a tonnage of books devoted to these prickly bushes and, increasingly, on specialist websites.

But a rose on the printed page or computer screen is but a paltry thing compared with its wondrous living self, hence the enormous value of HRG membership. Its programme of UK days out and occasional overseas tours opens the gate to many a private collection that would, in most cases, be impossible for the general public to see. The group was founded in 1990 by members of the Royal National Rose Society who share an interest in wild (species) and cultivated (hybrid) roses of historical importance, including many no longer widely grown.

The HRG's president, retired high-flying advertising boss Michael Charlesworth, says that one word sums up the unique quality of these old roses: 'charm'. Walking around his Somerset garden, I was keen to discover his personal much-loved favourite. 'That's a bit like asking someone to nominate his favourite picture or piece of music,' he says, but I push him to name one. 'Then it has to be the Gallica "Charles de Mills", a wonderful example of a classic old rose, with impeccable form, purple-to-deep-red colour and exquisite perfume – the perfection of a sumptuous old rose, despite its uncertain origin.' Another?

'For its stunning camellia-like form and bright pink complexion and heavenly perfume I'd choose the Bourbon "Louise Odier", bred in France more than 150 years ago and still going strong. What's more, she flowers perpetually, dispelling the myth that old roses do not bloom continually throughout the summer.' And your indispensable climbing rose? 'Ah, "Mme Isaac Péreire",' he says without

Gallica 'Charles de Mills'

hesitation, 'another Bourbon – once seen and smelt, never forgotten.'

Fortunately, each of Michael's faves is easily sourced in garden centres and specialist nurseries, but only through the HRG's network of followers will the more obscure beauties be found. As with all horticultural societies, members swap cuttings, plants, seeds and information.

The HRG's members also receive its bi-annual *Historic Rose Journal*, with articles about lesser-known rose gardens and collectors alongside mailings with vital information about its programme of modestly priced events. One such that I'm already signed-up for is a lunch and guided tour by Noel Collum of her outstanding collection of roses at Clinton Lodge in Sussex, followed by a private evening visit to Sissinghurst led by its head gardener, Troy Scott Smith. Sign up for membership now at historicroses.org – a gardener cannot better spend £15.

KITCHEN GARDEN
SIMON COURTAULD
ASPARAGUS

Although readily available in most supermarkets throughout the winter, I do not wish to eat asparagus from Mexico or Peru. 'To everything there is a season... a time to plant and a time to pluck up that which is planted': that time in Britain is early summer, May and June, and it is well worth waiting for. We were lucky enough to inherit an asparagus bed when we moved here ten years ago, but when planting new crowns it is advisable to wait two or three years before taking a crop. The ones which I planted five years ago are still not producing as many shoots as those which may have been in the ground for twelve to fifteen years. When the season ends – supposedly at the time of the summer solstice – the asparagus stems left uncut will produce tall ferny foliage, and sometimes red berries, which will feed the crowns for next season and should not be cut down until October, when the greenery turns yellow.

Asparagus has long been cultivated in this country: Samuel Pepys was very partial to it, referring to asparagus gardens in London – and was then more commonly called sparrow-grass. The wild asparagus, which looks not unlike samphire, grows in sandy soil near the sea, but is more usually seen on Mediterranean coasts. White, blanched asparagus is much

favoured in European countries, but the green belongs to Britain.

The joy of eating asparagus fresh, within an hour or two of being cut, is hard to describe, but it is important that it should not be overcooked. Older recipe books recommend boiling for up to fifteen minutes, but in my experience the asparagus stems, laid flat in a pan, should not need more than about five minutes in boiling water. I have noticed that television chefs, for some unaccountable reason, always peel the outer skin of the stems, which can only take away some of their flavour.

The classic way of eating asparagus is with the fingers, dipping the tips in melted butter or hollandaise sauce, or – recommended to me last year – in a soft-boiled egg (as in toast 'soldiers') or an egg fried in butter. There is of course, the malodorous urine factor, but it's a small price to pay for this annual treat.

COOKERY
ELISABETH LUARD
STRAWBERRIES

No need to remind season-savvy oldies that home-grown asparagus and field-ripened strawberries are flavours of the month of June. Not a moment to lose: the season starts in May and by mid-July it's all over. With asparagus, keep it simple (see Kitchen Garden, above). As for strawberries, the Italians make the most of theirs with a drop of Modena balsamic. Spain likes to cut the sweetness with the juice of a bitter orange. In Britain, strawberries are unthinkable without cream, whipped or otherwise, preferably with meringue. The French dress theirs up in a *tarte aux fraises* – as do I.

Meanwhile, just to balance the books after all that butter and cream, help is on hand in Anne-Lise Miller's *Too Young to*

Grow Old (Fisher King, £14.99). All you need to know about liver-detox, genetic modification and the microwave.

Strawberry tart with lemon cream
This is an easy version of *tarte aux fraises* as sold in every patisserie worthy of its Saturday queue in France. The pastry is a rich almondy shortcrust and the fruit is laid on a squishy bed of lemon curd lightened with crème fraîche. Assemble the tart just before you're ready to serve. On a hot day, chill the butter for the pastry in the freezer.

Serves 6–8

The pastry
75g plain flour
1 tbsp ground almonds
75g chilled unsalted butter
1 tbsp icing sugar
1 egg yolk
The filling
1 jar lemon curd (about 350g)
about 150ml crème fraîche or thick strained Greek yoghurt
500g strawberries, hulled and halved lengthways
To finish
3-4 tbsp redcurrant or other berry jelly

Make the pastry first. Sift the flour with the ground almonds into a bowl. Grate the butter into the flour and toss lightly to mix. Using just the tips of your fingers, rub in the butter till the mixture looks like fine breadcrumbs.

Sprinkle in the sugar. Bring the crumbs together with the egg yolk forked with a little cold water till it forms a softish dough ball (work it as little as possible). Wrap in clingfilm and leave to rest in a cool place for half an hour or so. Then roll it out to fit a 22cm tart tin with a removable base. Prick the base, line it with foil and weight with a few dried beans or a spoonful of uncooked rice.

Bake the tart-case for 20 minutes in a pre-heated oven (350F/180C/Gas 4), then remove the foil and bake it for about 10 minutes more, until the pastry is nicely golden and set. Remove the sides of the tin and leave the case to cool.

When you're ready to serve, fold the crème fraîche or yoghurt into the lemon curd and spread it over the pastry. Top with the halved strawberries, cut-side up in concentric circles. Give the fruit a shine with warm red currant jelly melted with a little water.

'Getting stroppy with the receptionist is just not going to help.' The distinguished oncologist Karol Sikora talks to *John Sutherland* about useful strategies for cancer

Try to make your doctor like you

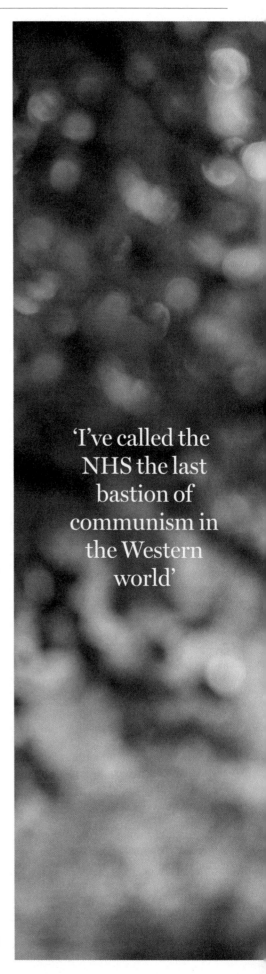

'I've called the NHS the last bastion of communism in the Western world'

Professor Karol Sikora is among Britain's most eminent oncologists, with a long history of front-line engagement with a disease that will, over the course of our lifetimes, afflict one in three of us. He has headed research teams and hospital departments in Britain and elsewhere, and for two years led the World Health Organisation's cancer programme. He has also written twenty books, the latest of which is *The Street-wise Patient's Guide to Surviving Cancer*, published in June. Here he talks to John Sutherland, emeritus professor of English literature at University College London, about the practical steps patients can take to make a difficult experience more bearable.

Sutherland: Congratulations on an informative, comprehensible and witty manual. The topic is of obvious interest to people like me who have an unwelcome personal acquaintance with all those technical terms ending in 'oma' – sarcoma, lymphoma, carcinoma, etc. Your book opens with two instructions. The first is 'control your treatment'. The second is 'come to terms with the fact that the NHS is, as its name proclaims, serving the nation's health, not yours particularly'. Could you enlarge on this advice?
Sikora: We all love the concept of the NHS and often treat it as a religion. Unfortunately, it has no incentive to

move into the far more consumerist world that we are used to everywhere else. Buying a budget air ticket, getting internet shopping or even getting a pair of new glasses is a lot easier than getting a GP appointment or advice about a worrying symptom. I've called it the last bastion of communism in the Western world. The paradox is that it can provide the best care in the world for the majority of its customers, often with fantastic personal care, but not always. The main message of the book is that by taking control of your own destiny you can ensure you get the best out of the system and not lost in its many blind alleys, which is easily done in a world of targets, rationing, delays and under-capacity. Become an informed consumer and not a service user.
Sutherland: How handicapped in getting the best treatment is the 'oldie'? Is there a covert *triage* at work? After all, the successful treatment of a baby with a hole in its heart is giving someone another seventy years of life. On the other hand, 'Uncle Tom Cobley's had a good run, let's offer the old chap palliative treatment'. If that's the unstated calculation (and of course it is *maybe*), how does the older person with cancer confront it? And overcome ☞

Karol Sikora, right: 'Convince your doctors that you enjoy life and want to continue'

it? Or must he simply take it as it comes? Kismet.

Sikora: Rationing abounds, but political correctness insists the NHS is not ageist. Doctors now have to do mandatory training every year – I was proud to score 100 per cent in my equity and diversity course. I've framed my certificate and put it in our guest room toilet. It's all madness of course – doctors have always looked after all patients whatever their age, colour, creed or sexual persuasion. The problem is that the cost of many cancer drugs is astronomical. Would you really want us to spend £100,000 on a new cancer drug for a 95-year-old with severe dementia for two months of increased survival in a care home? If you do, then what services do you want to cut? That's the dilemma society just can't face. With motor insurance we price older people out of the system – should we do the same for healthcare? If I'm a political party with that policy, you're not going to vote for me.

My advice is to convince your doctors that you enjoy your life and want to continue, and perhaps more importantly that you are willing to accept the inevitably increased risks of certain treatments as you get older. After all, you are only as old as you feel.

Sutherland: You tell us that you used to think it was a 'war' against cancer – one that I remember Richard Nixon declaring 40 years ago. Now you see it as a 'cancer industry'. Can you explain? Has the 'war' been won?

Sikora: The military metaphors remain – magic bullets, targeted therapy, collateral damage. But the emphasis is now on control rather than the destruction of cancer cells. After all, if we can control a 72-year-old's cancer for a decade they will reach their expected lifespan of 81 years. That's the way the war is going – a negotiated settlement.

Sutherland: I am 77 years old. Six years ago I had a radical prostatectomy. PSA, last time it was checked, was undetectable. If there is a recurrence – it happens – would my medical practitioners think me 'worth' a drug such as Provenge, which you tell us costs £98,000 for three months' treatment? And works, apparently.

Sikora: Let's hope your PSA stays down. Provenge was never licensed in any European country and its US manufacturer has gone bust. It was hyped out of all proportion and gave only

Sutherland: 'Would my medical practitioners think me "worth" an expensive drug?'

a few weeks survival benefit at great cost. But there are about five similarly priced new drugs available. That could mean that the treatment of a prostate cancer that has spread could reach £500,000 by 2020. That would bankrupt all healthcare systems, not just the NHS. We have to find better ways to ensure we all benefit from medical innovation.

Sutherland: You make the point that most cancers are survivable. There are, you say, 200 varieties. Which are the pussycats and which are the bastards? And which respond least well to delays in the system, once diagnosed?

Sikora: As long as a cancer remains localised to its site of origin it can be cured by surgery or radiotherapy. The problem is cancer cells spread by the lymphatic system and the blood stream. Chemotherapy doesn't care where the cancer is located and is unfortunately only partially effective for most common cancers – lung, breast, prostate and colon. That's our big problem. So detecting cancer before it spreads has to be our main priority to improving outcomes. This means earlier diagnosis and speedy treatment pathways.

Sutherland: You stress good manners as a policy in the patient's search for the best treatments and the best medicine. Good manners – and flowers for the receptionist. Can you enlarge?

Sikora: The NHS is a people business. Most of its staff are dedicated and remarkably caring. And they naturally respond well to pleasant patients. I've sat in our waiting room and observed wonderful interactions. But things go wrong, delays occur even in the best places. Getting stroppy with the receptionist is just not going to help. I've seen people shouting and swearing. Remember, just because you have cancer doesn't mean that life's other tribulations will end. You won't find a car park slot, you'll still get speeding fines, your children may still be unreasonable. But if someone is particularly helpful be appreciative – everybody likes positive feedback. Telling someone they have a lovely smile costs nothing. The lower down the food chain you are the less you get thanks in the NHS – that's where the unsung heroes are to be found.

Sutherland: If the worst comes to the worst, what can the medical profession do for someone whose days are numbered? And what can one do for oneself? I was struck by the gallant way Oliver Sacks confronted his death sentence: multiple metastases of the liver, a recurrence from nine years before of a melanoma of the eye. As Sacks wrote in the *New York Times*, 'It is up to me now to choose how to live out the months that remain to me. I have to live in the richest, deepest, most productive way I can.' What advice would you give a patient in Sacks's terminal condition? You must have had to do it often enough over your long and distinguished career.

Sikora: Everybody faces this situation very differently. The prediction of when death will exactly occur is notoriously difficult. So my advice is: do what you want to do, make peace with relatives you have fallen out with, travel while you can to see places you've always wanted to see, and above all don't get absorbed by detailed monitoring of your disease's progress.

I've had several patients who have willed themselves to stay alive for a specific event – to survive their wife, to get to their daughter's wedding or to see their first-born. Not all made it, but it has taught me how complex the human body really is. While we can reduce the body to molecules with modern science, we will never fully understand either the mind or the spirit. ◍

The Street-Wise Patient's Guide to Surviving Cancer by Karol Sikora is published by EER Guides, £14.99

Still With Us

Tom Lehrer

Michael Barber celebrates the nonagenerian iconoclast, long retired from singing and songwriting.

Tom Lehrer giving a rare interview at his Californian home in early 2000

According to the historian Arthur Schlesinger Jr the 1950s were the most humourless period in American history. Unless he was making a distinction between humour and wit, Schlesinger overlooked the mordant songs of his fellow Harvard alumnus Tom Lehrer, who at 88 is still, in his own words, 'sliding down the razor blade of life'.

Lehrer began performing at a time when 'there were certain things you couldn't say in front of a girl'. But he was equal to the challenge. Sixty years on there is still something wicked – in every sense – about lines like this from his Boy Scout riff 'Be Prepared': 'Don't solicit for your sister/That's not nice/Unless you get a good percentage of her price.' He also rhapsodised about necrophilia and masochism, and wrote a jaunty Revivalist hymn in praise of

nuclear apocalypse: 'Oh we will all fry together when we fry/We'll be French fried potatoes by and by ...'. No wonder *Time* denounced him as 'un-American', and the *New York Times* warned that 'Mr Lehrer's lyrics are not fettered by such inhibitory factors as taste.'

A great admirer of W S Gilbert, Lehrer struck a chord in Britain when it was revealed in 1957 that Princess Margaret was a fan. Reassured by this, the BBC played some of his less-offensive songs and his first LP became a must-have for embryo satirists like Richard Ingrams, who described him as 'a real breath of fresh air. We sang all his songs – they were very provocative. Lehrer was a genuine satirist, well ahead of his time'. He did a brief sell-out tour here in 1959 and later contributed to *That Was the Week That Was*.

Five years younger than Ingrams, I too became a fan, without realising

quite how inflammatory Lehrer's lyrics were. Consider *I Wanna Go Back to Dixie*, in which he says 'I wanna talk with Southern gennl'men/Put my white sheet on again/Ain't seen one decent lynchin' in years ...'. It never occurred to me that were Lehrer to sing this in, say, Little Rock, Alabama, he might well be lynched himself. In fact he was careful not to push his luck, choosing venues where he could be sure of a liberal, literate audience. The nearest he came to physical assault was in San Francisco at the hands of the devout Mexican film star Ricardo Montalbán, incensed at his mockery of 'modernised' Catholic ritual in *The Vatican Rag*: 'Do whatever steps you want if/You've cleared them with the Pontiff ...'.

Someone else who, like me, discovered Lehrer as a teenager, compared him to Roald Dahl: they both had an edge that delighted kids and disturbed their parents. 'The nastier the sentiment, the wider the smile,' Lehrer told Sir Cameron Mackintosh when Mackintosh was putting on *Tomfoolery*, a celebration of Lehrer's songs.

From a privileged rag-trade background in New York, where his father made neckties, Lehrer was a mathematical prodigy who entered Harvard in 1943, aged fifteen. By then he was also an accomplished pianist who liked to parody popular songs and by the time he began to study for a doctorate was in demand at student parties and local nightclubs. His first LP, a privately pressed edition of 400 copies, spread 'like herpes' far beyond the Harvard campus, and eventually, after several re-pressings, sold more than 350,000 copies.

Fame beckoned, but Lehrer wanted it on his own terms, saying 'What good are laurels unless you can rest on them?' The thought of having to sing the same songs night after night appalled him: 'It would soon become very boring. I don't crave the anonymous affection of an

'I don't crave the affection of an audience. Royalties are what I want'

audience. Royalties are what I want,.' not applause.' Aged forty, having written 37 songs, he gave up performing. A few years later Henry Kissinger was awarded the Nobel Peace Prize, after which, as Lehrer famously said, 'political satire became obsolete'.

Lehrer never had to sing for his supper. Although he failed to complete his doctoral thesis, he taught maths for forty years, first at Harvard and MIT, latterly at the University of California at Santa Cruz, where he also gave a course in musical theatre, revealing an unexpected passion for Rodgers and Hammerstein. He never married either, and so could do as he pleased. Recalling how his class soon learned not to quiz

him about his fifteen minutes of fame, a student of his said he was 'one of the most private people I've ever met', a verdict Lehrer did not dispute. He was mightily relieved to have done so little prime-time television, thus minimising the risk of being accosted by strangers.

To me, his catchy ragtime melodies and pithy lyrics, delivered with sardonic brio, are still as fresh as when I first heard them long ago. But it's a mark of how far the liberal consensus has shifted that in some circles he is now considered politically incorrect. Could it be because, in 'My Home Town' he describes someone as 'the village idiot'? – surely a mild epithet given that he 'liked to burn down houses just to see them glow'. He himself explained that he gave up writing songs once it became apparent that 'audiences wanted to be exhorted rather than amused', adding that what he really cared about was 'old-fashioned things like nuance and the challenge of finding a rhyme, which don't seem to matter any more'. More's the pity. ◍

'We're going to need a lawyer, George'

Penny Mortimer smoked for 55 years – despite Cherie Blair's disapproval – until a hypnotist came along

Farewell, my lovely fags – or is it au revoir?

On 12th July 2017 I had not smoked a cigarette for one whole year.

A year earlier, two months before I turned 70, I visited a hypnotist in Swiss Cottage, London. She talked to me for three hours; it wasn't any of the stuff one associates with hypnotism – the counting up and down or the clicking of fingers. She droned on a bit and then I left, having been told to crumble my remaining cigarettes and throw them in the bin.

I started smoking when I was 14. I had joined the local badminton club, and a girl of 16, named Beth, took me into the back room and taught me how to do it 'properly'. It wasn't pleasurable but I thought it was what would nowadays be called 'cool'.

My mother then smoked about ten cigarettes every evening, and I would pinch a couple from her packet and go and milk the goats on our pig farm. The stench in the goat shed easily masked the smell of tipped Gold Leaf.

After university, I came to London. It was the end of the 1960s and almost everybody seemed to smoke – just like in *Mad Men*, where Don Draper and the rest of the crew chain-smoke throughout.

When I was 24 and pregnant with my first daughter [the actress Emily Mortimer], I went to see an eminent gynaecologist in Harley Street. On his desk sat a packet of twenty Player's cigarettes and a gold lighter. Spotting these, I said, 'I suppose I'd better stop smoking, had I?'

'Oh no,' he said. 'I mean, you could cut it down a bit, if you wanted to. It might make the baby a little smaller, but we don't like big babies.' If a doctor said that today, he or she would be struck off.

As the anti-smoking lobby grew more vociferous, my rebellious streak grew. My husband – John Mortimer, the writer – and I were invited to dinner at Chequers,

almost a year to the day after Labour won the 1997 election, before the smoking ban was introduced.

It was a beautiful May evening and about 16 of us were standing on the terrace, surrounded by 1,200 acres of fresh Buckinghamshire air. I had heard that Cherie Blair did not allow smoking in the house – the house where Winston Churchill smoked his cigars, where politicians from behind the Iron Curtain and trades union leaders puffed on their roll-ups. Standing next to her on the terrace, sipping my glass of champagne, I said, 'You won't mind if I smoke out here, will you, Cherie?'

'Well, I'll allow you just one, if you really have to, Penny,' she said, 'But it is a filthy habit.' So I lit up one in either hand.

Other people weren't putting up with the aggressive, self-righteous anti brigade. At that time, a well-known theatrical agent was lunching at his usual table in The Ivy restaurant in London.

When the coffee arrived, he lit a large cigar and was puffing happily on it when an American man at the next table picked up his glass of water and doused the cigar. The agent didn't remonstrate

Smokin' Penny Mortimer, London, July 1969

but calmly paid his bill, lit another large cigar and, as he left, stubbed it out in the American's risotto.

I derived a fair amount of pleasure from smoking – so why did I give it up? I'm not sure. A couple of years ago, I suffered a burst appendix and was ill for a long time, spending long periods in hospital. Of course, one isn't allowed to smoke in hospital but this didn't cause me much anguish. Still, every time I came out, the first thing I did was light up a cigarette and, from then on, chain-smoke. When I was bedridden at home, I was getting through two packs a day – cigarettes were a great comfort.

But, after I started to return to normal life, I began to think about the inconvenience of the habit. When my daughters were staying with me, they didn't allow me to smoke in the house because of the harm to their children. It didn't cut me any slack when I told Emily that, when I was breastfeeding her, I smoked Gitanes, and she has since only ever been in hospital to have her babies. After my daughters' smoking ban, a neighbour came into my conservatory, in deep midwinter, and fell about laughing at the ridiculousness of seeing me, huddled up in my mink coat, puffing away.

I was shocked to find my forty fags a day cost £7,500 a year. Then a friend told me they knew someone who had given up a three-pack-a-day habit after seeing a hypnotist. I made the appointment and here I am today, smoke free.

Am I happy? I am pleased I have the willpower to quit, and delighted that I no longer have a cough and that there are no dirty ashtrays in my house. But I have to admit I do miss it sometimes and feel envious when I see people lighting up.

I quit smoking when I was almost 70. As there probably won't be much else to look forward to, I think I will take it up again when I'm 80 – if I get that far. ◐

BIRD OF THE MONTH

The Puffin

BY JOHN McEWEN * ILLUSTRATED BY CARRY AKROYD

Where the small burn
Spreads into the sea loch
I found the mad, clever clown's beak
Of a puffin.
How many times
Had it whirled into its burrow
With six-fold whisker
Of tiny fishes?
How many times
Had it grunted love
To its parrot-faced lover?
Norman MacCaig, from *Puffin*

It requires a pilgrimage to see seabirds, so the cutest-looking member of the auk family, the puffin (*Fratercula* – little friar – *arctica*), is the only one in the top ten most popular UK birds list. Penguin's Puffin books for children, launched in 1940, prevail; and oldies will remember Lundy island's puffin stamps – Lundy is the anglicised *lunde*, the bird's Norse name.

The collective noun is a circus of puffins. The carnival-mask beak acts as a spade for digging the nest burrow – assisted by sharp, raking toenails – and can hold and catch fish simultaneously; 61 sand eels and two rocklings is the incredible record. In winter, when puffins roam the seas, geolocators reveal they can travel thousands of miles from their breeding grounds. The beak's bright carapace is shed, the tear-like eye-nicks disappear. Airborne, they can whizz along at 50mph; but water is their domain. Adam Nicolson's two-part documentary *The Last Seabird Summer?* (BBC4, 2016) on the Shiant Islands (bought by his father) in the Minch, hauntingly illustrated the contrast when the seabirds' return transforms emptiness into teeming life. Nicolson writes adoringly of puffins in *The Seabird's Cry* (Collins, £10.99)

Puffins congregate in rafts and mate offshore and then re-possess their immemorial nesting grounds. Carry Akroyd once spent a week on the Isle of May: 'We used to see the puffins lined up along the clifftop, looking out to sea, and called it "going past the bus stop". One morning, there were none. We went over to the other side of the island and there they all were, looking the other way because the wind had changed.' A proposed wind farm in the Forth now threatens May's birds.

From March through August, puffins are ashore. They can live more than thirty years, and nest in warrens, sometimes co-exisiting with rabbits, the turf so laced with their burrows that it sometimes collapses. A single egg is laid in May. Incubation takes six weeks and, for a further six, the young puffling is fed underground – protected from predatory gulls but not rats, often the scourge of seabird colonies. It is then abandoned. Goaded by hunger, it walks down to the sea in the safety of night and does not return for two years.

Papal dispensation once allowed puffins to count as fish in Lent. They are still eaten in Iceland and elsewhere. The writer David Profumo prefers their gamey red meat to guillemot, but found to his regret that day-trippers do not qualify for a drink at St Kilda's Puff Inn. There are occasional London appearances: one was found wandering Sloane Square in September 1984. UK numbers are in decline but not on the Shiants, where a £900,000 extermination scheme (half EU-funded) has recently rid the islands of rats. St Kilda has the UK's largest puffin colony.

On the eve of what would have been his 80th birthday, *Elisabeth Luard* discovered lost photos of Cook from 1961, when she worked with him at The Establishment Club

Peter's friends made the 60s swing

DOCTOR JONATHAN MILLER HAS GONE TO THE THEATR

For just two years in the early Sixties – mid-1961 until the end of 1963 – The Establishment Club in Soho was the hottest ticket in town. For those of us who worked there, it was the beating heart of the universe.

What a thrill it was to find this cache of unpublished photos from the Establishment's archive – particularly on the eve of what would have been Peter Cook's 80th birthday, on 17th November.

The cache of press photos, commissioned by the club, had been stored unopened in a box in various Luard attics and garages – in Spain, the Isle of Mull and Wales – since 1963, when the club closed.

Before 19 Greek Street became London's first (and last) satirical theatre-club, it was the Club Tropicana, a strip joint with rooms. The advantage to the proprietors, Peter Cook and Nicholas Luard, was the disreputableness of the area, the space – two long, thin rooms with a warren of smaller ones behind – and the proximity to Theatreland and the politicians in Westminster.

Sean Kenny, designer of the minimalist set for *Beyond the Fringe*, was recruited by Peter to strip out the velvet curtains in favour of floor-to-ceiling blackboard paint, industrial lighting and wall projections of Ban the Bomb marchers. In the basement, Annie Ross sang Christopher Logue's subversive lyrics to Tony Kinsey's jazz quartet, until Dudley Moore took over at the piano.

Upstairs, the ladies bar doubled as an art gallery, dominated by Gerald Scarfe's enormous cartoon of a semi-naked

Harold Macmillan, mostly in green. Photographer Lewis Morley rented the top floor, where he snapped Christine Keeler straddling a heart-shaped chair, to publicise a film about the Profumo affair.

Nightclubs are never appetising by day. The fragrance that hung over the scrubbed wooden tables and unmatched chairs when I arrived at midday for work (mornings I spent at art school) was vinegary Chianti, leftover shepherd's pie, Balkan Sobranies and untipped Gitanes.

By night, the ultra-fashionable membership – seven thousand on the night the club opened – was diluted with a shifting cast of poets, conmen, artists, playwrights, actors, professional drunks, bent policemen and East End villains.

I was there the night Peter persuaded the Richardson twins, rivals to the Krays, not to trash the upstairs bar, talking them down the stairs and on to the street – an act of astonishing bravery – with a wildly improvised account of Sir Arthur Streeb-Greebling's heroic attempts to teach ravens to swim underwater.

The green room doubled as the waiters' changing-room and (briefly) accommodated *Private Eye*, before new editorial premises were found three doors along the street. The move left me, the secretarial help, behind, in Accounts with unglamorous Mr Platman from Southend – not what I had in mind. What I had in mind was the less famous but equally glamorous of the two proprietors, Nicholas Luard (reader, I married him – it wasn't an easy forty years, but what did I expect?).

The monotony of office work was relieved by – my choice – marketing forays on Cambridge Circus for the *Eye*,

often with the assistance of 'Professor' Irwin Corey, a club regular. The prof's sales technique was to roll up a trouser-leg, revealing a hairy shin, a yellow sock held up by scarlet suspenders, and rush into the traffic, waving the limb and shouting. As soon as an alarmed driver rolled down a window, it was my responsibility to thrust the mag through the gap and demand payment. Success was limited.

The main hazard of life at the club for a day worker was negotiating the green room on the way to and from the office. On a regular day, it might be just the cast – the two Johns, Fortune and Bird, always-tranquil Eleanor Bron – agonising over a script. Or it might be Barry Humphries's alter ego, Les Patterson, eating fish and chips; on stage, Dame Edna (then just

The Establishment, 1961. Back row: four staff, including manager Bruce Kopp and barman Brendan; Owen Hale (lighting); John Bird; Jeremy Geidt (actor). Middle: Nick Luard; Peter Cook; David Walsh (actor); Carole Simpson (singer); John Fortune; Steve Baker (carpenter); unknown. Front: Dudley Moore; Sean Kenny (club designer); Wendy Snowden (Cook's first wife); unknown

Mrs Everage) and her gladdies died a premature death.

Even more alarmingly, Frankie Howerd – told about my previous status as a deb – stood to attention in string vest and ragged underpants and addressed me as my namesake, The Queen.

The regular Establishment show began at 9.45pm, amid a clatter of clearing plates. But there was sometimes another at midnight, when Peter came in from the show. *Beyond The Fringe* was still running to packed houses at the Fortune Theatre.

I had seen *Beyond the Fringe* soon after it opened, and there was never any doubt that Peter, then in his mid-twenties, was the star. It helped that he was absurdly handsome, tall and slender, with a mop of dark hair and bright, watchful eyes. Of the performers – lanky Jonathan, earnest Alan, bouncy Dudley – Peter was the one throwing ad-libs and spanners in the works, scanning the audience, gauging responses.

On stage at the club, wearing a Macmillan mask with gestures to match – or embroidering on the unholy activities of his Order of the Leaping Nuns at *Private Eye* – this alertness remained.

London in the Sixties. Days of wine and roses. No shortage of wine; not many roses. Sex was easy, at least for the men. As for the women, we were the first generation liberated by the Pill, but we hadn't yet worked out how to say 'no'.

Some of us had read Simone de Beauvoir, a few of us Anaïs Nin. Not all of us were looking for husbands, some of us were looking for life. Which was why I went to work at *Private Eye*, around issue ten, for a fiver a week.

Soon, the magazine needed a new proprietor capable of paying the print bill. The Establishment and its youthful entrepreneurs, Cook and Luard, were the logical candidates. The editorial team at the *Eye* – Richard Ingrams, Christopher Booker and Willie Rushton – were unwilling to risk identification so soon in

Cook in Harold Macmillan mask, outside the Establishment (formerly Club Tropicana), 1961. Cook often lampooned the PM. Right, with club co-founder Nick Luard, 1961. Cook eats the Lord Chamberlain's document that censored the revue script

negotiation. So they decided to dispatch the anonymous office girl, me, to request permission to sell the mag at the club, a sign that co-operation might be possible.

Once safely inside the club – no need for membership if you were a personable young woman in a Mary Quant miniskirt – I headed for the office at the back, where I found the two proprietors answering telephones. I asked whether we could sell *Private Eye* in the club.

'Sure,' said Nicholas, absent-mindedly waving a cigarette. 'Go ahead.'

Peter was not so sure. If *Private Eye* viewed the Establishment as a bunch of Cambridge lefties promoting pornography, the Establishment saw the *Eye* as a bunch of Oxford schoolboys purveying lavatorial jokes. But, still, the marriage was made, if not in heaven.

Thereafter, I spent most of my evenings at the club, tucked into the projection room with a bird's eye view of audience and stage. That's where I was on the night an overly-refreshed Siobhán McKenna, outraged by Peter's crucifixion sketch – the one where the central figure ascribes his elevation to a very influential Father – grabbed the offender by the tie and dragged him from the stage. Or maybe it was irreverent mention of the IRA that caused the trouble.

Most revolutionary of all was Lenny Bruce, brought to London by Peter. Lenny, quite simply, was magic. Romantically good-looking, hopelessly addicted to substances none of us had even tried, he could say the unsayable, and did.

While the public schoolboys of our generation were dismissive of women and fearful of the mysterious bits between our legs, Lenny treated us as equals. Hard to believe that this was a time when women couldn't get a passport or a mortgage, or open a bank account, without a man.

To Lenny, if war was obscenity, sex was pure joy, and women were the source. On stage, he came straight to the point: 'Listen up, folks. If f**king is truly an act of love and procreation, why don't we say, "Un-f**k you, mister?"'

Hard to imagine it now, but there were no barriers – intellectual or physical. No velvet ropes or pistol-packing minders; no such thing as celebrity. On any evening in the club, Bertrand Russell might be arguing a philosophical point with Arnold Wesker. Or James Butler, son of the then Home Secretary, might be discussing the catering in French jails with 'Dandy Kim' Waterfield, fresh from Fresnes slammer. Or Nicholas's childhood friend Edward Adeane, later Prince Charles's Private Secretary, reminiscing about raptors with hawk-fancier Ken Loach. Or the artists' model Henrietta Moraes, fresh from romancing Lenny Bruce by locking him in the green room with a syringe, flirting with Lucian Freud.

It all came to an end too soon, when the money ran out. The original Edinburgh *Beyond the Fringe* show was bankrolled by Willie Donaldson, a Wykehamist like Nicholas, and a minor co-performer with Peter at the Cambridge Footlights. While Willie was kept financially afloat by a flotilla of ship-owning maiden aunts, Nicholas soon ran out of his grandfather's legacy. So Willie topped up the Establishment's coffers when needed and dropped a ladleful of money into *Scene*, Nicholas's short-lived arts magazine.

Published weekly – never mind that Tom Stoppard was its theatre critic (pseudonym: Henry Boot) or that the news pages carried the first national press on The Beatles – *Scene* sank with all on board, and took the Establishment Club down with it.

Still, for a short while, the Establishment encapsulated the real revolution of the Sixties – the social and generational mix-up that was at once cultural, political and physical – and we didn't even know it.

But that was then and this is now. You'd never get away with it today – or would we? Might be worth a try. ◑

Elisabeth Luard is author of My Life As a Wife: Love, Liquor and What to Do About the Other Women *(Bloomsbury, £16.99)*

Maureen Lipman protests at being infantilised by increasingly irritating and inane Health and Safety announcements

I am NOT a child

In my day there was much talk of infantile paralysis – a bleak prognosis among childhood illnesses. It meant iron lungs, iron boots and years off school. Its medical name was poliomyelitis, abbreviated to polio. Today, in the aftermath of its blessed eradication in all but three countries, I'd like to reclaim the term 'infantile paralysis' for the way – thanks to Health and Safety – I am being made, daily, to feel.

Increasingly, inanimate objects issue directions at me in warm, mellow voices like a slightly dotty friend. The lift tells me lovingly that the doors are about to close or open, whether I'm going up or down and what I might expect to find when I reach my floor. I've been known to mutter, 'Shut up, you're a lift.'

My bus stop now digitally alerts me to the right bus. On the Tube or a train, the mellow voice advises me to 'Mind the gap', to be wary of unclaimed packages and look back at the rack above my seat to make sure I have taken all my belongings. The voice is that of my late mother, only missing the flat vowels and the threat of a hanky with spit on it.

It makes one feel quite gaga and utterly without common sense. All right, I did leave my pashmina in the overhead rack and I do have cranberry flapjack in the corner of my mouth, but I don't want some voiceover actor, who earns more than I do, telling me off about it.

To add insult to injury, they've now painted two feet on the escalator steps – a left and a right foot – in case a grown person who's been standing on escalators since she was on solids isn't sure which way to face while travelling upwards.

My satnav talks down to me. Well, it has done the Knowledge, after all.

'Right at next junction... No, I said right... And round the scary roundabout and up the stairs to Bedfordshire... you have reached your destination, check your teeth for spinach. Turn off the engine, pinhead.'

WHOLE ALMONDS

500g ℮

WARNING
May Contain Nuts

If you want really helpful instructions, buy a carton of juice. The printed guidance on my smoothie is beyond useful; it's overfamiliar. 'Hi! I'm your strawberry, raspberry, passion-fruit, kale and Jerusalem artichoke, five-a-day friend! Lick me, suck me, let me slide down your throat and you'll grow thick hair and pert breasts in seconds...'

'Bog off!' I think. 'I have friends of my own and you're a carton!'

Its promises only get more ardent. It promises to taste good and do me good and never use concentrates or preservatives. 'Concentrate on how preserved you feel now,' I tell it. 'In the wheelie bin, you wet, cardboard harlot.'

Have you checked the back of a packet of almonds recently? It will say, 'beware. This product contains nuts!' Or a packaged Stilton? 'This cheese can kill! Do not consume if you are pregnant, or allergic to dairy or James Blunt.'

> 'The estate agent, whom I've never met, rings cheerily: "Hi, Maureen. Tommy here. How ya doin'?" How am I doing what? Pulling my knickers up?'

The situation is less clear in lavatories. Do you now turn a tap, press a tap or waft your hands around beneath the taps to satisfy the 'please wash your hands' sign. If the temperature takes you by surprise, you might have missed the very small notice saying, 'beware! water very hot!' Now you must fathom the drying of those clean, lightly burnt hands. Do you hit the dryer repeatedly underneath? Or do you thrust both hands downwards into the hand-shaped gaps and watch your ancient skin fly off the bones of your hands like long johns on a washing line?

Is the machine which looks like a dryer in fact a dispenser? If so, is it the type with paper towels dispensed in stacks of nine or ten which drop to the floor ('beware this floor is wet!') in a clump? Or the kind with a sheet of scratchy paper that descends, nicely torn, via a handle? It's all trial – and mostly error.

It isn't just inanimate objects that infantilise me. The estate agent, whom I've never met, rings cheerily: 'Hi, Maureen. Tommy here. How ya doin'?' How am I doing what? Pulling my knickers up? Going to school on my own? 'Very well, thank you, but Mummy says I'm not to speak to strange estate agents. Goodbye.'

And don't get me started on 'pop', as in 'Just pop in here, dear, pop your clothes on the back of the door, pop on this gown, then wait in the waiting room until I can pop you in to see doctor.'

Am I imagining I'm being talked down to? Perhaps it isn't patronising prattle but genuine concern? I resolve to meet the world with the warmth and friendliness that it metes out to me. Then I find myself on a train.

'This weekend, the hour has changed,' says the mellow voice, 'which means it may be darker than usual when you return home at your usual time. Please take care.' Once again, Health and Safety has endangered my health and safety by sending my blood pressure rocketing. ◊

We know the Easter story. But what about all the figures in biblical and classical pictures? *Laura Freeman* gives her gallery tips

How do you read religious paintings?

What's the story? That's the question to ask, standing in front of the great paintings of the Bible, the saints and the classical myths and history. Who's he? And she? What happens next? How does it all end?

Some stories are easy. Man, woman, snake, apple. That's Adam and Eve in the Garden of Eden. Temptation followed by Fall. Others are more difficult. I remember standing flummoxed in front of a painting by the German artist Johann Hulsman in the Fitzwilliam Museum in Cambridge, racking my brains for which bit of Ovid has a young woman talking to what looked like Mr Toad dressed up as a washerwoman.

It turned out to be Latona and the Frogs, showing the moment when Latona, mother of Apollo and Artemis, transforms peasants into frogs for stopping her drinking from their lake. Latona isn't one of the big, sexy stories – Pluto Abducting Proserpine... Venus and Mars... sleeping Samson and scheming Delilah – and mostly appears in ornamental garden sculpture.

Stories matter. 'The older painters took their subjects seriously,' wrote Kenneth Clark, patron saint of the BBC's *Civilisation* (recently reincarnated as *Civilisations*) and the wartime National Gallery. 'They always wished the spectator to believe that the incidents they depicted had really happened and were still worth remembering.'

When Sandro Botticelli painted *The Adoration of the Magi*, or Leonardo da Vinci *The Last Supper*, or Caravaggio Salome wincing as the head of John the Baptist is brought to her, it was to bring those events vividly, startlingly to life.

Clark, writing in 1974, was already worried that such stories were being lost. 'It comes as a shock to an elderly man,' he wrote, 'to find how many biblical references have become completely incomprehensible to the present generation.'

Gabriele Finaldi, present director of the National Gallery, shares some of Clark's concern. Last year, he told me, 'If we are not familiar with the great themes of classical antiquity and the Bible, if we are not aware of the background, then our experience is impoverished.'

How, then, to enrich it, particularly at the time of a crucial religious festival such as Easter? What to do if your *Odyssey* is shaky, your Old Testament worse, and you can't tell your Peters from your Pauls?

Start with the right attitude. I used to feel defeated in front of religious paintings. Once I'd worked out the obvious ones – Annunciation, Crucifixion, Last Judgment – I'd give up and go to the gift shop.

'Why make a puzzle over it?' says the dreary academic Mr Small in Mary McCarthy's novel *Birds of America*, lecturing one of his pupils in the Sistine Chapel. What Michelangelo really cared about, says Small, was line, form, colour, not 'those old Bible tales'.

'You're so wrong, Mr Small,' says Peter, one of his bright-eyed students. 'Michelangelo wanted to say something. I haven't got the whole message yet, but it's there.'

Do make a puzzle over it. Start with the figures and setting. Is this the loose-togas and peeking-nipples world of classical gods and goddesses? A place of centaurs and satyrs and booze-ups with

Bacchus. Or is this noble Rome? Senators speechifying, Caesar in triumph, Tarquin bearing down on Lucretia...

Or the desert landscape of Nativities, Flights into Egypt and Massacres of the Innocents?

Be strict. Look at the painting first, have a best guess about who they all are and what they're up to, look for clues in costume, gesture and symbols, and only then check your answer with the wall text.

Cheat a bit. In my first term studying history of art at university, I did a quick job of filling the (vast) gaps in my knowledge with the *Usborne Illustrated Children's Bible*, Roger Lancelyn Green's *The Tale of Troy* and Ted Hughes's seductive *Tales from Ovid*.

Get yourself a spotter's guide. James Hall's *Dictionary of Subjects and Symbols in Art* is a beautifully written gazetteer that sorts Ariadne from Arachne, Joseph from Job. We can tell saints by their attributes, often a symbol of their martyrdom. Poor old St Agatha is shown carrying her breasts, cut off as punishment for her Christian faith, on a silver salver. St Lucy carries her eyeballs

for similar reasons. St Anthony Abbot, less gruesomely, appears with a pig, which kept him company in his exile in the wilderness.

Beware of jumping to conclusions. Skinny scholar in a hair-shirt vest, with lapdog lion? St Jerome's a safe bet. Gym-bunny beefcake wrestling a lion? That's Hercules. Weeping youth among a dozen lions? Try Daniel in the lions' den.

Start spotting this Easter with paintings from the Passion – the cycle of paintings devoted to the events leading up to and following the Crucifixion.

St Anthony Abbot with his pig, in Piero di Cosimo's *Visitation* (c 1489-90)

Work it out piece by piece. First, Christ on the cross. At his feet: the Virgin Mary, in blue, perhaps in a swoon; Mary Magdalene, often in red, her long hair loose, holding an unguent jar; St John the Evangelist, a handsome man, consoling the Virgin or clasping his hands in prayer (not to be confused with John the Baptist, who wears a sheepskin gilet and carries a lamb).

Either side of Christ, on their own crosses, are the Good and Bad Thieves. These are the 'bandits' captured and crucified on the same day. On the hard ground of Golgotha, the site of the Crucifixion, Roman soldiers cast lots. These men, in Roman military dress, throw dice for who can claim Christ's tunic. In some paintings, a nesting pelican pierces its own breast to feed its young – a symbol of Christ's sacrifice to save our souls.

In paintings of the Descent from the Cross – the Deposition – you find Joseph of Arimathaea, a finely dressed member of the Sanhedrin (Jewish council), who asked the permission of Pontius Pilate, Roman governor of Jerusalem, to take down the body of Christ. Nicodemus,

a follower of Christ, more modestly dressed, is seen pulling the nails from His feet.

Renaissance artists with a flair for the dramatic often include two more women (an excuse for elaborate dresses, hats, scarves – a painter's delight) fainting, weeping and praying, as in the *Descent from the Cross* by the Master of the St Bartholomew Altarpiece (c 1500) in the National Gallery.

Paintings of the Resurrection on Easter Sunday show Christ rising from the tomb as Roman soldiers sprawl sleeping at his feet. One of the loveliest paintings in the Passion cycle, on the morning after the Resurrection, is the '*Noli me tangere*' – 'Touch me not' – scene, which has Christ, disguised as a gardener, drawing away from Mary Magdalene who kneels in amazement before him. In Titian's imagining, Christ carries a hoe. In other versions, he wears a gardener's sunhat and even pushes a wheelbarrow.

Sometimes you'll be stumped. Keep looking, keep puzzling. If you ever lose confidence, remember: 'I haven't got the whole message yet, but it's there.' ◍

ACE CULTURAL TRAVEL

Holidays for the culturally curious

aceculturaltours.co.uk
01223 841055

ATOL 10204 ABTOT 5237

Portrait of a woman, possibly Maria Trip, Rembrandt van Rijn, 1639

On The Road

'I'm a hopeless traveller'

David Attenborough has travelled the world but yearns for his own bed. By *Louise Flind*

You've travelled all your life – is there anything you can't leave home without?
My front door key. It has little charms on it that my dear wife, Jane, gave me.

What do you really miss from home?
I'm very fond of my bed.

Favourite holiday destination?
To be absolutely truthful, I'm a European and I like European things. I like European breakfasts, climates, people, architecture and music. Holidays, as far as I was concerned, were for kids. You got to know them a bit better. I suppose the last holiday I really had was with Jane and that's about twenty years ago.

Would you ever lie on a beach?
That's not a holiday – that's a purgatory.

Where did you go on your honeymoon?
Isle of Wight – that was all I could afford. I thought we had to go overseas, and that was as far as we could manage at the time.

Do you like being away from home?
I liked going to new places when I was in my thirties and forties, but now I'm in my nineties home is where I want to be. This is where I'm happy. I've got all the things and the people I love around me. I've ticked a lot of the things I was desperate to see and I've seen them. I'd like to see them again and I'm not against travelling, but I love home. I love sitting surrounded by books.

Hotel, apartment or igloo?
Most recently for 'Blue Planet', we went to Trinidad to film leatherback turtles, and we stayed in a very un-atmospheric, concrete, tropical tourist place.

What is the strangest place you've ever slept in?
Probably in a woodcutter's hut in a very remote part of Paraguay. We were in the middle of a huge rainstorm. Unexpectedly, with no maps, we came to a clearing and there was this hut. The woodcutter said we

Home boy: David Attenborough

could sleep in the store room. Anywhere that was dry would have been wonderful. There was a wooden shelf and a couple of planks over huge earthenware pots. As I lay there, I heard a strange, rustling noise. I found a torch, and the wall alongside me was covered with a shining, moving carpet of cockroaches.

There was also a hideous stench of dried, smoked fish – that was what was in these big pots and what the cockroaches lived on. I don't mind cockroaches at all. I don't like rats. I've had rats running over my face in bed in Fiji. The rat in the loo was in rather a posh place in India.

What about diseases?
I'd been living away for four months in long houses with Dayaks in central Borneo. Getting back home was wonderful: crisp sheets and my dear wife. Exhausted, I went to bed and woke up drenched in sweat and thought, 'This is it – this is malaria – this is what you always dreaded.' So I woke up my poor wife and said, 'Excuse me, I've got malaria, what do I do?' While I was wondering what to do, I put my hand on the sheet and it was red hot. While I was away, Jane had bought an electric blanket with dual control. Mine was on all night – I was absolutely parboiled. What a relief.

Favourite animal?
Most of the animals I've brought back went to the zoo. The nicest things we had were bush babies. They're like monkeys with very big eyes; nocturnal and so, so sweet.

We set up a room with hollow logs and had fourteen babies over a period of years. They were just enchanting, but not for cuddles. For cuddles, we had monkeys. We had a little, woolly one called William. William would escape and run down to the laburnums in the garden and sit laughing at me. I knew how to get him back. I would sit on the bench and start cuddling my daughter, Susie, who was about six, and William would get extremely angry and come belting across and insert himself between us.

Do you get emotionally attached to the animals?
You don't become emotionally attached to centipedes or lungfish.

Strangest thing you've ever eaten?
Caterpillars in New Guinea.

Biggest headache?
The biggest headache used to be that you'd go away for three months, making 16mm films, but there was no way of seeing any of it. Once in Paraguay, having sent some film back after eight weeks, we received a cable saying, 'Regret to tell you but there's a hot spot on the long-focus 200 mill lens.' A hot spot is when it burns out in the middle of the picture. All the close-ups we'd taken were write-offs.

Have you been sad to leave a location?
I once lived on a small island halfway between Fiji and Tonga, in the Lau Islands. We lived there for several weeks, making a film about Polynesian village life. It was an idyll; the people were lovely and you lived exactly as they did, in a thatched hut. Every morning, we speared fish on the reef for breakfast.

Top travelling tips?
No – I'm a hopeless traveller, really. I wouldn't offer anybody tips. I'm pampered. I recommend travelling with a film crew really. They solve all your problems for you. 🌕

Enchanting Bruce Chatwin told 'the truth and a half' in dazzling style. He died at 48, before reaching his prime, says his biographer, *Nicholas Shakespeare*

The Byron of travel writers

Chatwin and St Nicholas Church in the Mani, where his ashes were scattered

Interviewed in Australia, 17 years after his death at the age of 48, I was asked by a puzzled young journalist: 'Who was Bruce Chatwin?' It was a reminder of how few things in life are more perishable than literary fame. Only a short while before, this English writer had been a cult figure, and not merely in Australia.

'You would suppose Lord Byron had died,' wrote James Lees-Milne on reading Chatwin's obituaries in January 1989. Many people had felt a sense of loss out of all proportion to their expectation.

Published posthumously, Chatwin's collected journalism, *What Am I Doing Here*, topped the *Sunday Times* bestsellers list. A bookshop calling itself Songlines, after his most famous book, opened in Berlin. In Genoa, an annual travel festival/prize was established in his name, with street-wide banners advertising the *Premio Chatwin*. Try to imagine this recognition being accorded, say, to Martin Amis, or any contemporary English writer, come to that. It's hard.

The German anthropologist Michael Oppitz had known Chatwin in Nepal, and reckoned that, through his life, Chatwin had given a new definition of the Writer as Hero. An icon of the backpacker, Chatwin inspired a myriad young people to set off and live in Calcutta or Patagonia – 'and then come back with a diary that no one publishes'. Today, Chatwin's signature black Moleskine notebooks

– which he purchased from a single stationer's in Paris – are on sale in almost every major city.

For all this, the author who popularised them has become oddly erased. 'Does anyone read Bruce Chatwin these days?' mused Blake Morrison, reviewing his collected letters in 2010.

He was, of course, everything the English distrust. Stylish. Passionate. Good-looking. 'There are few people in this world who have the kind of looks which enchant and enthrall,' said Susan Sontag. 'And Bruce had it. It isn't just a beauty; it's a glow – something in the eyes. And it works on both sexes.' And a charmer – 'He was out to seduce everyone,' said Miranda Rothschild, who once went to bed with him. 'It doesn't matter if you are male, female, an ocelot or a tea cosy.'

But he was a lover of theory and of the French; and obsessive, which we dislike in particular.

Perhaps that's why it has taken a polymathic European like Werner Herzog to continue to see Chatwin's point. Herzog's new feature-length documentary on Bruce will be part of the BBC's re-minted *Arena* in 2019. For Herzog, Chatwin's significance remains undiminished.

'When I think of Bruce Chatwin now,' he told me, 'I think of the ultimate storyteller. It's the resonance of the voice and the depth of his vision that makes

him one of the truly great writers of our time.'

You have to reach back to Joseph Conrad, Herzog believes, to find a comparable figure.

To his friends, Bruce was more than a writer. 'He was one of the two funniest people I've known,' says Salman Rushdie (the other being Christopher Hitchens). 'He was so colossally funny you'd be on the floor with pain. When his stories hit their stroke, they could simply destroy you.'

Bruce told Colin Thubron, 'I've always loved telling stories. It's telling [rather than writing] stories, for what it's worth.'

To an unusual degree, Bruce's stories involved their listener. 'He made you participate in what, in that moment, did not seem to be a fantasy,' said Francis Wyndham, who in 1972 had recruited him to the *Sunday Times*. 'One was included in it, even though he did all the talking. But he made me feel he was talking because of me, which explained the sense of exhilaration.'

This certainly described my experience. I was 24, recently returned from the southern tip of South America, where I had read his first book, *In Patagonia*. Back in London, I sought him out.

In those days, I kept a diary. On 19th January 1982, I wrote, 'The morning with Bruce Chatwin, after eventually locating his Eaton Place bedsit: a bicycle against the wall and Flaubert on the floor. He was younger than I imagined, rather like a Polish refugee: baggy-trousered, emaciated, grey-blonde and blue-eyed, sharp-featured and razor-worded.

'He has just delivered a manuscript – a novel about a square mile near Clyro where two families fight, without exposure to the modern world, through two world wars. He talks like a bird, very funny, very boyish and very well-read.

He said to me, "Isn't it extraordinary how the most fraudulent people often have a very good eye for the genuine article?"'

I laugh to think of the image I had of the author before I met him. From *In Patagonia*, I constructed a silent observer whose longest sentence was 'I see'. In fact, he told me later, 'I'm at my happiest having a good old yakking conversation.'

Only afterwards did I meet the lady in Patagonia who confessed, 'Don Bruce, he talked a lot, *bastante* [too much].'

Or, in Alice Springs, a woman who complained: 'He murdered people with talk.'

He didn't stop yakking from the moment I entered his tiny attic flat. Within minutes, he had provided a telephone number for the King of Patagonia, a pipe-smoker who ran the free faculty of law in the Faubourg Poissonnière. As well, he gave me numbers for the King of Crete, the heir to the Aztec throne, and a guitarist in Boston who believed he was God.

In return, he wanted to know about Argentina. Flattered, I told him a story I'd picked up in Salta, about a figure called Güemes, a hero of Argentina's independence who had lent his colours to the famous gaucho poncho: black for the death of Güemes, red for the blood of his soldiers. Güemes, I'd learnt, was an hispanicisation of the Scottish Wemyss: the colours were those of a Wemyss tartan.

At this, Bruce's eyes widened and, speaking in italics, with his hands waving, he explained how he was at that moment at work on a theory about the colour red.

Did I know that Garibaldi, while fighting for neighbouring Uruguay's independence, had filched a consignment of these ponchos from a warehouse in Montevideo and, on the ship back to Italy, had tailored them into the uniforms for his 'redshirts' – and so inspired the red flags flying over the barricades of revolutionary Europe and ultimately the Kremlin?

Bruce had a talent for making others see the world through his eyes. That day, I left his flat taking reasonably seriously the link between a Scots tartan and the red flag of Socialism.

In our subsequent meetings, I swiftly realised that telling stories was how he gave of himself.

'He was looking for stories the

An auction-house education: Bruce Chatwin, 20, working at Sotheby's, 1960

world could give him and that he could embellish,' says Rushdie, who travelled with him through central Australia. 'He didn't give a damn whether they were true or not; only whether they were good.'

To Bruce, who was very theatrical but also deeply serious, a good story was a true story. His storytelling engaged all his faculties, his youthful looks, his savage mimicry, his peacock voice... I still remember his piercing screech, during a walk near his house in Oxfordshire, after he came up with a title for a well-known contemporary's next novel: *Kissing the Wrist*.

He found the English literary establishment asphyxiating ('Boy, you know when you've been patronised by X'), in large measure because he had not been to university. He was 26 when he became a mature archaeology student at Edinburgh, and he didn't last the course.

Educated in the auction room at Sotheby's, and then on long travels in pursuit of nomadic tribes in the Sudan, Afghanistan and West Africa, he was an autodidact who gravitated towards other autodidacts – such as Paddy Leigh Fermor, with whom he stayed in

the Mani in Greece (where Chatwin's ashes were scattered) while writing *The Songlines*, and the Australian novelist Murray Bail, his travelling companion in India. He would have agreed that precisely what qualifies these and other of our best travel writers – Robert Byron, Norman Lewis, Colin Thubron – is the lack of a university degree.

More than most authors, and reflecting the insecure impulse of the self-taught, Bruce felt the need to eyeball the people he wrote about, go to the places and read the books (often in the original Sanskrit or French).

Paradoxically, for someone often unjustly accused of being a 'whopper merchant', he did not have an inventive imagination. He had the imagination to tell stories – to connect them, to enlarge, colour and improve them – but not to invent.

'A storyteller of bracing prose, at once glass-clear and dense'

'His art of arranging, composing and enspiriting the material was, though, more like a novelist's than a journalist's,' says his American editor, Elisabeth Sifton.

That, for my money, is why his work stands to last. At his best, he is less economical with the truth than spendthrift. He tells not a half-truth, but a truth and a half. As Sifton puts it, 'Bruce was an artist, not a liar.'

Hans Magnus Enzensberger was another European polymath who 'got' Bruce. 'In psychological terms, Chatwin suffers from *Beziehungswahn* – a delirium of establishing connections.'

In that sense, as I told the Australian interviewer who had never heard of him, Bruce was a precursor of the internet, a connective superhighway without boundaries, and with instant access to different cultures. A storyteller of bracing prose, at once glass-clear and dense, he offered a brand-new way of representing travelling. And he held out in his six books the possibility of something wonderful and unifying, inundating us with information but also with the promise that we will one day get to the root of it.

'He posed questions that we all want answered,' said Robyn Davidson, another of his innumerable friends, 'and perhaps gave the illusion that they were answerable.'

When Chatwin died 30 years ago of AIDS (probably contracted from his Australian lover, Donald Richards) on 18th January 1989, he brought down the drapes on an era; soon after, the Iron Curtain fell, replaced by the worldwide web. What Bruce, who hated computers, would have made of the internet age, is hard to say.

He might have grown to resemble his description of Herzog's favourite actor, Klaus Kinski, playing the Viceroy of Ouidah: 'a sexagenarian adolescent all in white with a mane of yellow hair'. He might have become a boring Ancient Mariner like Samuel Taylor Coleridge. Or he might, as I like to think, have fulfilled his potential as one of the finest English writers of the past century.

Rushdie put it best: 'Bruce had just begun. We didn't have his developed books, the books that might have come out of falling in love with his wife [Elizabeth Chanler, whom he married in 1965 and remained married to until his death]. We saw only the first act.' ◉

BETTMANN/GETTY

Age cannot wither your style, says *Peter York*, if you follow his rules

How to look good after sixty

My grandmother, inexplicably brought up in France – though as British an old bundle as they come – once said she didn't want me to grow up like a Frenchman.

'Why not, Granny?'

'French men [very, very long pause] wear scent.'

I decided that I would wear it because it sounded Frenchy, fun and was granny-banned. I have a shelf full of the stuff now, even though it's one of the things women in research say they hate absolutely about a man 'preceded by an overbearing cloud of cologne'.

Ever since, I've been guilty of what Bertrand Russell said of Anthony Eden: 'He's not a gentleman; he dresses too well.' Some say I look 'dapper'. In Sloanespeak, that means a putdown combination of trying-too-hard-airhead-what-are-you-compensating-for-plus-worse. It echoes the idea that being foreign in any way is non-U – because all kinds of French or Italian men completely get the idea of good clothes as an expression of educated, bourgeois knowing about the world. Put a bunch of well-educated, well-paid, senior, English, corporate types alongside their Paris or Milan counterparts and you're squirming for your nation.

It chimes, too, with the old English double-bluff of affecting not to notice clothes and never making an effort. Old Brits *do* make an effort – when there's a uniform involved, from black tie on.

The older you get – and if you've hit seventy like me – the more loaded the whole 'dapper' thing gets. When should you stop enjoying your nice clothes and go out looking like a bundle intended for landfill?

Here are my rules on how to look tolerable over sixty:

Don't wear excitable, sports-derived clothing. That includes lurid trainers, hoodies, sweat pants, Lycra cycling kit or anything that young people wear when doing sporty stuff. It's unseemly, whether you've got a Dad bod or not.

Don't wear tight clothes or anything intended to show off your assets. Don't wear ultra-skinny trousers or bum-freezer jackets.

Don't wear music-derived outfits in imitation of your musical heroes – mid-period Bruce Springsteeny jeans and leather bomber jackets, or Iron Maiden 1982 tour T-shirts.

Don't wear pointy shoes, square-toed ones or those elfish, turned-up toes.

Don't wear a beard (though hipsters have made all that complicated now), don't do a Trumpoid comb-over and don't have a grizzly ponytail. Don't dye your hair bright black, brown or old-rocker blonde. And don't be mahogany, permatanned (people now just think skin cancer). I never did any of these things. I used to cover punk gigs wearing Brooks Brothers pure prep – button-down Oxford shirt, linen jacket etc. Punks – often very design-sophisticated – completely got the fact that I was playing about with the symbolism.

Clothes are a conversation, where their wearers are saying things not just about themselves, but about the state of the world; and how they feel about different dress codes.

Conventional, upper-middle opinion loves to call this 'poncy', meaning things they don't get but instinctively fear aren't class-correct. 'Poncy' means pretentious and pointlessly overdone; too considered. They're right sometimes – expensive 'fine dining' is full of ponciness – but sometimes it's just dissing anything ambitious and original.

Wear moisturiser I use something cheap from Boots called E45 in large

pump-action containers. It never occurred to me this could be an un-English activity.

Keep as many of your original teeth as possible for as long as possible. Barring accidents, it's not that difficult. If they migrate or fall out, your face changes shape in worrying ways.

Lose the belly Unless you're ill ('It's my glands, doctor!'), there's no excuse. It's a public offence to have a giant belly, and dangerous, too. It's seriously easy to gain weight and not that hard to lose it, either. I don't go to a gym and I wouldn't, unless a doctor made me. The more you drink – and I love it when I'm out – the more careless you are about the joy of artisanal bread rolls, pasta and novelty macaroons. If I gave up drink, I'd get tremendously thin, never look pink or loopy and think better. But drink adds interest to events and people, which could otherwise be a bit boring.

Wear timeless clothes I'm currently wearing my 25-year-old Cordings corduroy suit. It's made of a cord so thick and delicious it'd stop a bullet. It's 'teamed with' – as fashion people say – a hyper-cheap, pink, linen shirt from Uniqlo – so cheap I bought four; plus Crockett & Jones plain vamp shoes in shiny deep brown.

Yesterday, I was wearing a nice, plain – no brassy buttons – navy blazer in Loro Piana fabric from Volpe, Pimlico's finest menswear shop. Over a Ralph Lauren, forest-green, cable-knit, cashmere crewneck bought from Madison Avenue just pre-crash, when I was feeling delusionally flush. Over an old Pink's, made in Ireland, red-striped shirt.

And natty, check trousers – very modestly priced – from H&M, the Ikea of global outfitting. Tasty.

Don't have plastic surgery It sounds completely brilliant, until you see the results on famous people who have had all the good advice big money should get you. Think Mickey Rourke... or Barry Manilow. ◍

Peter York is co-author of 'The Official Sloane Ranger Handbook' (Ebury Press)

The Sitwells were celebrated writers. But Sachie, *William Sitwell*'s grandfather, was unfairly overshadowed by Edith and Osbert

Three of an unusual kind

The 2nd October 1988 was an unusual day for me. Thirty years ago, I arrived for my first day at university – at the seemingly bleak, red-brick-and-concrete campus that was the University of Kent.

A little ambivalent about the way my life was moving, I hadn't thought to visit the place before starting life as a student there. It was my 19th birthday and I literally didn't know anyone. And the day before, my grandfather had died.

Across every newspaper that day were obituaries of Sir Sacheverell Sitwell. His owl-like features peered out of the pages, his thin lips betraying what I knew so well as a wry smile that could at any time erupt into a fit of giggles. There were acres of newsprint about this man of poetry, this last sibling of a great literary trio. This wonderful man was known to me and close friends and family as Sachie. It is a strange moment when one's family name is spread across the papers.

But here I was at this bleak, modern establishment – a world away from the ancient buildings, cloisters, traditions and uniform of my previous dwelling, Eton (which was partly the point, to widen my horizon).

I knew no one to console, cheer or chat to me about the fact that – having been dropped off by my mother some hours earlier and checked into a room that felt less homey than a prison cell – my grandpa had died yesterday. And he wasn't just any old grandpa.

For it had been mine – and my siblings' – privilege to get to know Sacheverell Sitwell in his final years, after we moved into a wing of the home he lived in after his wife, our grandmother Georgia, had died, eight years before.

That house is Weston Hall, Northamptonshire, where I now live. The desk I sit at in his old dressing room was his desk, at which he wrote his 130 books, as well as newspaper articles and pamphlets of privately published poetry.

Sachie's output was exhaustive. He wrote on the forgotten painted monasteries of Bucovina in Romania, the art and culture of Japan, the story of English furniture, and studies of the works of Liszt and Mozart. He wrote poems about picking blackberries, or the irritating buzz of a fly as it knocked against a window on a hot summer's day. From newspaper columns – such as Atticus in the Sunday Times – to his books, he showed a prolific, detailed, exacting and ego-less knowledge and interest in the world, its peoples and its art.

But he was the quietest of the siblings. And he remains today a little underrated, his writings less studied and analysed than theirs.

Edith had her rings – aquamarine stones adorning her almost spookily long fingers. She wore capes and cloaks, vast hats and, as Elizabeth Bowen said, she resembled 'a high altar on the move'.

And there was Osbert – flamboyant, confidante of royalty; bitchy socialite; controversial essayist; famous satirist of his own family. Through his own multi-volumed autobiography, he created one of the most famous characters in literary non-fiction – his father, Sir George Sitwell.

According to Osbert, he invented a revolver for killing wasps and an egg made of condensed milk. He commissioned a herd of cows that were dulling his view to be painted

Edith, Sir George, Ida, Sachie and Osbert, by John Singer Sargent (1900) Below: Sachie, Edith and Osbert (1962)

Sachie's mind was extraordinary. His books are filled with the names of gypsies and princes, and details of temples and cities. Even in old age, his mind darted about during conversation.

'Did you know there was a shop in Ootacamund that sold Dundee cake... I once met a lavatory attendant at the Café Royal called Sigmundo Pandolfa Malatesta, who was descended from the tyrants of Rimini.'

Born in 1897, he once told an interviewer, as he neared his late eighties, 'It's wonderful to be alive.'

At that age, he would sit in a chair in the drawing room at Weston, surrounded by copies of his own books on the floor. He puffed on Silk Cut cigarettes, smoking them like cigars, rather than inhaling deeply.

He couldn't pronounce 'th'. 'I heard really v most fearfully funny fing v uvver day...'

He would tell a joke and descend into schoolboy giggles.

I suppose he got a little dotty towards the end of his life. His polite way of saying he was bored with someone's company would be to say: 'You will come back and see me again before too long, won't you?'

He might say this three minutes after a visitor arrived.

A local writer once came to visit him. Over lunch, Sachie asked him: 'Do you know that frightful bore Simon Melville [not his real name]? He will not stop coming to see me v whole time.'

'Well, Sachie,' replied the guest, 'I am Simon Melville.'

He once slipped down the stairs while climbing them to bed – an ascent that always followed his announcement: 'I fink I might retire to my apartment.'

He sat there while help was called, wailing: 'Torment. Torment.'

Sachie was the only one of his siblings to marry, having fallen in love with a Canadian beauty, Georgia Doble, when she visited London in the 1920s. They had two sons, Reresby and then Francis, my father. The marriage effectively split the trio and Sachie spent the ensuing decades on his own work. Prolific, funny, extraordinary...

Having emboldened myself to enter the junior common room bar on that first night at Kent, I made some friends. They sang me happy birthday and we drank to the memory of Sachie. It wasn't such a bad start after all. ◐

with watercolour. He refused ever to dine with people as it 'interferes with the functioning of my gastric juices and prevents me from sleeping at night'.

And his relationship with his wife, Lady Ida, was so remote that he refused to clear a debt of hers in 1913. So she was sent to Holloway Prison for three months.

The press feasted on the shenanigans of Edith and Osbert and their frequent feuds with other artists and critics. The critics were gripped by Edith's *Façade* poems. Set to music by William Walton – early white rap, if you like – they were performed first through a curtain on a Sengerphone (an early, non-electric megaphone).

But Sachie was an intrinsic part of the trio. Like the others, he was dedicated to his work: art. With Osbert, he put on exhibitions of some up-and-coming

and hitherto unknown artists called Modigliani and Picasso.

'We did seem to be like rebels,' he once told me. And while he was never without a shirt, tie and a jacket, his – and his siblings' –rebellion was aimed at breaking their aristocratic mould. They wanted to pick up the pen, rather than the shotgun.

Sachie may have lived in the beautiful ancestral confines of Weston Hall (descending through a female line of the family since 1714, before Sir George acquired it from an aunt in 1898), yet he always fussed about money and kept to a strict timetable each day.

The floor of his dressing room was covered in piles of books and papers. No one was to walk down the passage while he was working. Gertrude, the housekeeper, could only clean the room when the couple were away.

Richard Davenport-Hines enjoys the latest edition of the DNB, with a growing cast of remarkable characters, every one an inspiration

Heroic lives

Hero worship is good for the character whatever one's age. Sociologists report that a deciding factor in whether adolescents of similar backgrounds become delinquent or not is their capacity for admiration. Those who look up to someone as a model – a relation, a sporting hero, a singer – tend to the good. Those who never learn to admire go to the bad. The same applies to grumblers in their sixties.

Each January, the *Oxford Dictionary of National Biography* (*ODNB*) provides my character-improving heroes. First published in 2004 in 60 volumes, and constantly updated so that it now includes about 60,000 lives, from Roman times to the age of Cameron and Clegg, the *ODNB* puts online an annual supplement of more than 200 short biographies of men and women who died four years earlier.

There are other *ODNB* supplements – to fill accidental omissions – and their eccentricities can be fun. Every dog-lover will enjoy the article last September on a tipsy Victorian baronet called Sir Everett Millais, who pioneered artificial insemination of basset hounds. But the January issue is always a reckoning.

In 2015 the dead of 2011 were commemorated. There are artists and authors, officers and officials, clergy and composers, criminals and police, surgeons, engineers, politicians and public nuisances. I spent several happy afternoons looking up people whom I knew and admired (inspiring military historian Richard Holmes), impressive strangers (such as Diana Lamplugh), those who gave my children pleasure (Ronald Searle and Dick King-Smith) and those about whom I was just plain nosey (the Ladbrokes bookmaker Cyril Stein and the political busybody David Hart).

The entry by Anne Pimlott Baker on Cyril Stein shows the *ODNB* at its best. It's a vivid character portrait of a man who epitomised the phrase 'hard but fair'. It catches the milieu of betting shops and casinos from the 1960s to the 1980s well too.

Simon Heffer is glorious on David Hart, known as Spiv at Eton, and blackballed by his own father when a candidate for White's Club. A failed screenplay writer and bankrupt property speculator, who bombarded Margaret Thatcher with policy papers, meddled in the miners' strike, but became persona non grata at Downing Street after telling the US Ambassador a whopper about a military communications system he was touting, Hart bounded back as a procurement adviser to Malcolm Rifkind, and as a dicey campaign manager for Michael Portillo's run at the party leadership.

There is little doubt which are the best articles of the batch – best not only because they are intelligent, worldly and generous, but because their subjects still seem important. Quiet wisdom brims out of Peter Parker's account of Harry Patch, the longest-surviving British veteran of the First World War (he died aged 111), and of the other veteran survivors Henry Allingham and Claude Choules. William Feaver has written an all-surpassing article on Lucian Freud. And in my mind

Have you seen my razor?

Are you having an affair?

GED

these are coupled with two excellent pieces on tragic women, Roger Philip Mellor on Kathy Kirby, and Chloe Govan on Amy Winehouse.

Parker describes Harry Patch advancing into action before dawn on 16th August 1917, and finding a young soldier ripped apart from shoulder to waist begging to be put down – an image that haunted him for 94 years. We learn of Patch's shrapnel wound in the groin, his grief for dead comrades, and 40 years of peacetime work as a plumber near Yeovil. He outlived two wives. One son was a drunkard who sold his father's medals to buy booze. The other son became estranged.

Patch never spoke about his war experiences until one night in his retirement home, just before his 100th birthday, a flickering fluorescent light awoke him with a jolt, and suppressed memories of the dazzle of being under shellfire came flooding back. Sought after for television documentaries, interviews and public events, Patch was resolutely non-militarist and non-nationalist: only in the last year of his life did he agree to join the British Legion after being bribed with a bottle of whisky. When he visited Langemarck cemetery, he put on a German war grave a wooden cross inscribed 'Comrades All. H P'. His recitation at Menin Gate of Laurence Binyon's famous lines from *For the Fallen* was deeply affecting.

Patch's modesty, pride in service, considerate manners, and mature dealing with fright are exemplary. He was an obscurity who became world-famous simply because of his longevity – and then proved to be admirable.

The contrast with Feaver on Freud is overwhelming. From early manhood Freud was always to be reckoned with. He inspired ardent love from his brilliantly exceptional children, and selfless devotion from his maîtresse-

From top, clockwise: Harry Patch, Lucian Freud, Amy Winehouse and Kathy Kirby

photographers who ambushed him, yet expected decent press coverage. Feaver lists his favourite food – woodcock, spinach, macaroons, nougat, deep-fried parsley – and mentions that he expressed 'his violent and occasionally irrational aversions by composing profusely offensive postcard messages'.

Then there is poor Kathy Kirby, born Catherine Ethel O'Rourke in 1938, whom the band leader Bert Ambrose waylaid at Ilford Palais. Ambrose became her Svengali and Lothario (she was 18 and he 60 when the sex started between them). He devised her image (an Anglicised Marilyn Monroe with dollops of lip gloss) and by 1964 she was England's highest-paid female singer, earning £40,000 a week.

After Ambrose's death in 1971, she found he had been a compulsive gambler who swindled her out of £5 million. She went bankrupt, went to a mental hospital, and on her release moved in with a lesbian fan who took her to bed and was later imprisoned for defrauding her of £30,000. Relying on alcohol and prescription drugs, Kirby slept in shop doorways, and was the unacknowledged aunt of the lucky sisters who married Lord Rothermere and Mark Thatcher.

As to Amy Jade Winehouse, born in 1983 and the youngest eminence to die in 2011, she began experimenting with self-harm at the age of nine when her parents divorced. She was fast on the road to ruin, undisciplined and churlish, working as a tattoo parlour receptionist when she got her first recording contract in 2002. Her throaty and beautiful voice, as much as the tragic lyrics, made her *Back to Black* the bestselling UK album of 2007. She already had signs of emphysema when she died of alcohol poisoning aged 27. *The ODNB* calls her an accomplished self-saboteur.

I find every mention of Freud compelling, and particularly his combination of severe working discipline with lawless impulses. And hearing Winehouse singing duets with Tony Bennett will convince any doubter that she had admirable gifts. It is easy to deplore a society that seems to prefer weak characters on auto-destruct, but perhaps one should celebrate a society that doesn't despise frailty. Anyhow, reading the *ODNB*'s annual tranche of strenuous, pushing lives nudges one into emulating the good, restraining the bad, and avoiding the pitfalls of the sad. ◑

en-titre, Lady Willoughby de Eresby. Any history of the late 20th century must consider his greatness as an artist – but also his social power. He mattered as much to the mood and character of London as Edward VII did to Edwardian England.

In 1941, Freud decided to try his luck on an Atlantic convoy, signed on as an ordinary seaman, sailed for Nova Scotia, was scared, frozen, bullied and ridiculed by the other seamen, discharged with tonsillitis and declared unfit for military service. Until he became super-rich, and the thrill of knife-edge risks became blunted because losses didn't matter, he was an obsessive gambler. 'He liked the decisive swipe, the emptying out, the utter exposure' of big bets just as his close friend Francis Bacon did. Money,

Freud said, was his 'ammunition'. He was glamorous and scuzzy by turns, but never gimmicky or submissive.

Feaver's character sketch stresses the animal in Freud, whose whippet Pluto shadowed him for 16 years.

'Doglike, consciously so, Freud favoured instinct over reason and appetite over inhibition; there was, for him, a sniffing out to be done and a watchfulness to be maintained in every situation.' Entering a restaurant or gallery in his trademark overcoat with silk muffler, Freud looked 'as wary as a fox scenting trouble'. Opening his front door in Kensington Church Street, 'he would greet with a quick inclination of the head and a baring of the teeth in a sniffy smile'. He was famed for cherishing privacy, kicked at

In 1980, *Gerald Scarfe* drew the titles for *Yes Minister*. The show never dates, thanks to the script and the brilliant actors

Westminster's cartoon comedy

In 1980, with pencils sharpened and sketchbook under my arm, I made my way to a BBC rehearsal room.

On the first day of rehearsal, things are always a bit edgy – some people don't know one another; others are old friends who have worked together before. When I arrived, the director, Sydney Lotterby, was already half an hour into rehearsal.

Sydney had contacted me to create the titles for a new comedy the BBC were working on called *Yes Minister*, written by Antony Jay and Jonathan Lynn. I thought, like others, that it was to be about the church. But now we all know it was a political satire based on the continuing battle between the government and the civil service. The first episode aired 40 years ago, on 25th February 1980.

It was probably because of my reputation as a political cartoonist for the *Sunday Times*, where I had worked for the past 15 years, having previously cut my teeth at *Private Eye*, that I was chosen. Sydney reasoned that, because of the political nature of the programme, having a real political cartoonist involved and making caricatures would lend the fictional characters credibility and make them seem like genuine 'flesh and blood' politicians.

On that first day, I watched the actors Paul Eddington and Nigel Hawthorne establishing their characters. I found Paul Eddington very friendly and forthcoming, but Nigel seemed almost shy and a little distant.

Having read the scripts, I knew that Paul's character,

'I have frequently found myself unable to think up things as funny as real events'

Jim Hacker, was a rather plodding, self-publicising minister and that Nigel would be the Machiavellian member of the civil service who would run rings around him.

In the show, British snobbery raises its nasty head. Sir Humphrey Appleby, Jim Hacker's Permanent Secretary, has a First in classics from Oxford's fictional Ballie College, while Hacker is a graduate of the London School of Economics. Sir Humphrey rarely misses an opportunity to bring this up. The third essential member of the team was the character of Bernard Woolley, brilliantly played by the late Derek Fowlds, who sadly died in January, aged 82. Bernard wears a tie from Magdalen College, Oxford. As the series progresses, Hacker becomes more knowing and cynical and uses some of Sir Humphrey's sly tricks himself.

In my political cartooning, I have frequently found myself, as Antony Jay said in the context of *Yes Minister*, unable to think up things as funny as the real events that happen.

Yes Minister and *Yes, Prime Minister* seemed to confirm what the public suspect is very close to the truth. For example, politicians are a wily bunch who won't answer questions. 'Let me be perfectly clear about this,' they say. What they really mean is 'Let me obfuscate and muddy the facts as much as possible.' The show capitalised on this brilliantly.

Nigel eventually became famous for delivering long-winded, grandiose, loquacious speeches peppered with technical jargon and wily dealings. His performance won him three BAFTAs.

Often when I start work, there is an awkward moment when I sit and confront my subjects – or victims – head on. Although actors are creatures who are used to being gawped at on stage and film, some can squirm under the artist's scrutinising eye. Being drawn is much more intrusive than being photographed 👉

Sir Humphrey, Bernard and Jim Hacker

'If it's any commendation, it was Mrs Thatcher's favourite programme'

or filmed, where a camera lens stands between the subject and the operator's enquiring eyes – especially when, as a caricaturist, I won't be 'picking their best features'.

In the past, I have sometimes found it difficult to draw actors because, strangely, they don't seem to have a character until they are acting a part. I can draw them in character but not in their own right.

A notorious example was Peter Sellers, who created the most wonderful characters – among them Mr Kite and Dr Strangelove – but personally could come across as rather bland. But *Yes Minister* would be different, because in it were the fictional characters I was to reproduce.

Sydney wanted the three characters to be animated for the title sequence. In true BBC fashion, there was very little money for the title sequence. Traditional animation, conveying movement by filming thousands of individual, hand-drawn and -coloured pictures, is labour-intensive, skilled and expensive. There are 24 drawings that flash before your eyes every second in a full-blown, Disney-type animation. That's not the sort of money BBC budgets can run to; so I had to use more economical animation methods. In fact, I had to do everything myself.

To achieve what Sydney wanted, I revived the rostrum-camera method I'd used for a previous film I'd made, called *I Think I See Violence All Around Me*.

The BBC booked me several days

Britannia meets Canute: Jim Hacker (Paul Eddington). *Right:* **Antony Jay**

Bernard Woolley, brilliantly played by the late Derek Fowlds, who died in January, aged 82. All pictures by Gerald Scarfe

in their rostrum-camera unit with the legendary Ken Morse, and I spent many laborious hours making drawings and photographing them by adding to them line by line.

The rostrum camera is fixed and points downwards towards the drawing board. I would begin the drawing with one pen stroke on the white paper. Then I'd take my hand away and click two frames of that line on 35mm celluloid film. Then I would continue and add to the existing line with another stroke, remove my hand and take another two frames, and then repeat the process, slowly building up the montage without my hand in shot. When the film was run at normal speed with no sign of my hand, the drawing appeared to be drawing itself, line by line – literally 'taking a line for a walk', as Paul Klee wrote.

Worryingly, this was a process where I could not see the end result, akin to the erection of a building brick by brick without plans. I wasn't

quite sure how it would end up or whether it would stand up. I could end up with Chartres Cathedral, or the Leaning Tower of Pisa – or a pile of bricks. Well, I think I got the Leaning Tower of Pisa. Not my best work but good enough, because the building-up process was apparently fascinating in itself.

I had no idea what a hit the show was going to be. Nothing is assured, especially in showbusiness. Sometimes what is apparently a highly successful package is put together and turns out to be a terrible flop. But a hit it was.

The titles became quite iconic, the show was brilliant and, thanks to the scripts and the actors, it hasn't dated at all.

I still get enquiries and requests for drawings from all over the Western world for any *Yes Minister* (which had 21 episodes, from 1980 to 1984) and *Yes, Prime Minister* (16 episodes, from 1986 to 1988) material. Some years ago, the opening title drawing of the three main characters was bought by a gentleman in Hong Kong.

If it's any commendation at all, it was Mrs Thatcher's favourite programme. I certainly feel very honoured to have worked on it. ◑

GERALD SCARFE

Was it The Last Hurrah?

When *Dafydd Jones* photographed bright young things 40 years ago,

Above: Boris Johnson at the Christ Church Ball, Oxford, 1985. *Below seated:* Hugh Grant, Marina Killery, Lulu Rivett-Carnac, Lord Neidpath and Catherine Guinness – at the Piers Gaveston Ball, the Park Lane Hotel, London, 1983

The Jeunesse Dorée of the 1980s at play

his sharp focus captured actors, writers – and future prime ministers

Above left: Nigella Lawson in a sedan chair, Dangerous Sports Club tea party, Gloucestershire, 1981. *Above right:* David Cameron in Bullingdon tails, Pitt Club Ball, Cambridge, 1987. *Below:* Jumping over a burning boat, Oriel College, Oxford, 1984

The inspirations for the writer's hit novel – and a new BBC series – were her father and her faithless lover. By *Selina Hastings*

Nancy Mitford's sad pursuit of love

The *Pursuit of Love*, published on 10th December 1945, was an instant and phenomenal success.

If ever there were a case of the right book at the right time, this was it. Funny, frivolous and sweepingly romantic, it was the perfect antidote to the long war years of hardship and austerity, providing an undernourished public with its favourite ingredients: love, childhood and the English upper classes.

Far more even than Nancy Mitford's previous novels, *The Pursuit of Love* – adapted for a new BBC series this spring – is intensely autobiographical.

The heroine, Linda Radlett, is beautiful, feckless and sensitive, one of the seven children of Matthew Alconleigh, an eccentric backwoods peer known for his defiant philistinism and the terrible force of his temper.

The hero is Fabrice – a portrait of Gaston Palewski, Nancy Mitford's lover, a French politician, known as Colonel, down to the smallest detail, from his demands to be entertained ('*Alors, racontez!*') to his habit of bursting into little snatches of song, and even the face he makes when knotting his tie.

But the character who dominates all the others, just as he dominates his own large family, is Lord Alconleigh, Uncle Matthew, a portrait of Nancy Mitford's father, Lord Redesdale, in all his glory, drawn with that devastating combination of caricature and unerring psychological accuracy which is one of Nancy's greatest gifts as a novelist.

Irascible, unreasonable and good-natured, there he is cracking his stock whips on the lawn, up at dawn and roaring at the housemaids, his eyes flashing a furious blue as he repeats his unshakable conviction that 'abroad is unutterably bloody and foreigners are fiends!'.

There is his favourite epithet 'sewer', his favourite records ('Fearful the death of the diver must be/ Walking alone in the de-he-he-he-he-epths of the sea') and his habit of falling asleep at the dinner table.

Although in middle age she became convinced that she had never been fond of either of her parents, Nancy's depiction of her father as Uncle Matthew is deeply affectionate. Frightening and funny, he is also endearing. Nancy was speaking her own mind in these words of Fanny's: 'Much as we feared, much as we disapproved of, passionately as we sometimes hated Uncle Matthew, he still remained for us a sort of criterion of English manhood; there seemed

Fabrice (Assaad Bouab) and Linda (Lily James) in *The Pursuit of Love* (BBC)

something not quite right about any man who greatly differed from him.'

Nancy wrote the novel from beginning to end in three months. Never before had she found a book so effortless to write, and never would she again. It was as though falling in love had given her access to a creative source of which previously she had barely skimmed the surface.

Evelyn Waugh read the manuscript, and it was he who suggested the title. Nancy's publisher, Hamish Hamilton, had no hesitation in declaring his enthusiasm for *Pursuit* ('the word brilliant has been used'). He recognised it as a winner from the first, asking for only a few, very minor, editorial changes: 'p. 252 – re Dunkirk. I know exactly what Linda means and I think she would probably have said it, but I have a hunch that Miss Mitford ought to tone down line 6. There are just too many people who didn't think it Heaven.'

His faith in Linda was amply repaid. The critics praised it – 'Highly diverting from the first to the last page'; 'More truth, more sincerity, and more laughter than in a year's output of novels'. The public bought it, read it and, it sometimes seemed, talked of little else.

It was the Book Society Choice for December, with 200,000 copies sold in the first 12 months. Hamilton had told her that in the end Linda might earn her as much as £750, but she made more than that (£798) in the first three weeks, and in six months over £7,000.

From all sides the congratulations poured in.

'Clever, clever Nancy,' wrote John Betjeman, 'I am proud to know you.' Uncle Matthew, whose opinion was

Love in a French climate: Nancy Mitford in Paris, 1956

awaited with some trepidation, 'sat with his nose in the book & grunted out various corrections: "Never got the stock whips in Canada, a bloke from Australia gave them to me" & so on. He was delighted with it but cried at the end.'

The opinion that mattered most was that of the book's begetter. Colonel was pleased with his portrait as Duc de Sauveterre, although constrained to point out that French dukes were not in life like that. 'He then introduced me to one & indeed he can hardly have been more like the late Harrington & less like Fabrice. Still – fiction.'

He had been flattered, too, by Nancy's dedication 'To Gaston Palewski' ('*Avec la dédicace, je dois entrer dans la gloire*').

But then, at the last moment, with the book already at the printer, he panicked,

frightened that the Communist opposition would scent a scandal in his association with *la soeur d'Unity Mitford, l'amie de Hitler*. There was a flurried exchange of telegrams between Nancy and her publisher – 'DELETE DEDICATION SUBSTITUTE LORD BERNERS', 'LEAVE GASTON IGNORE INSERTION PRINT AWAY' – before Colonel calmed himself and allowed the dedication to stand.

> ## 'The event she had been dreading for nearly 30 years: Colonel was married'

'*Please* never let Gerald [Lord Berners] know,' Nancy implored Hamilton. 'I count on you to be like a doctor & never tell tho it's almost more than I can expect.'

Much as Nancy had been gratified by Linda's enormous success, she could not feel happy while the cruel grey English Channel separated her (in England) from all she loved best in Paris.

Her own idea was to get back to the Colonel as quickly as possible, for not only did she miss him but she knew very well that if she were away from him for long, she would lose him.

There was that terrible roving eye of his, and she had been badly frightened by how hard she had had to work to re-establish herself after their year's absence from each other during the war. The Colonel was out of power now, General de Gaulle having resigned in January, and his future was uncertain.

When he did write or telephone, it always gave her joy. 'Your darling voice & your darling hand writing within an hour of each other is almost too much happiness. And I suppose the next best thing to having one's sentiments returned is to have them appreciated.'

But when she did not hear, she was miserable. 'Dear darling Colonel I think of you all the time – don't leave me for ever without a word of what is happening to you.'

She continued to live in Paris and love the Colonel for the next 25 years, until one morning in March 1969, when a small announcement appeared in the *Figaro*: '*Nous sommes heureux d'annoncer le mariage de M Gaston Palewski avec Violette de Talleyrand-Périgord duchesse de Sagan.*'

The event that Nancy had been dreading for nearly 30 years had finally taken place: Colonel was married. It was almost literally a death blow (she died in 1973, aged 68, of the cancer that first emerged in 1968), the bitterness of it exacerbated by the fact that Gaston's wife was a divorced woman. For years, Nancy had accepted the face-saving excuse that he could never marry her because he dare not risk his political career by marrying a divorcée.

Now retired from politics, he could marry where he chose, and his choice was not Nancy. ◑

Selina Hastings is the author of Nancy Mitford *(Random House)*

After a year of coronavirus, *Harry Mount* admired the divine result of another tragedy – Wren's City churches. Pictures by *Angelo Hornak*

Phoenix from the flames

My God, we had a terrible time over the year after the pandemic first struck. Over 100,000 people died in Britain alone.

It's not much consolation but things were much, much worse – for Londoners, anyway – 355 years ago, with the Great Plague of 1665-66, followed swiftly by the Great Fire of London in 1666.

The Great Fire did, though, produce the finest architectural achievement this country has seen: St Paul's Cathedral and the 51 City churches (88 were lost in the Fire), all by Sir Christopher Wren.

Deep tragedy caused exceptional beauty. Is it too much to hope for that an artistic genius will produce something similar, if not on such a magnificent scale, once our own pandemic is finally behind us .

Gothic St Dunstan-in-the-East; baroque St Vedast; the Doric Monument; St Bride's wedding cake; the Perpendicular fan vaults, St Mary Aldermary; Grinling Gibbons's cherubs, All Hallows by the Tower; St Paul's & St Augustine's

No architect before or since has had such a commission: to build so many churches and a cathedral. They were all built in Wren's long life – he died in 1732, aged 90. But, still, St Paul's was the first cathedral to be finished in its architect's lifetime – medieval cathedrals took centuries to build.

Appallingly, Wren was taken off the St Paul's job in 1718, aged 86. George I replaced him as Surveyor of the King's Works with a jobbing Palladian architect, William Benson.

In his late 80s, the sacked Wren walked along Cheapside to see his cathedral finished with a pointless stone balustrade. A distraught Wren declared that some people, 'like ladies, think nothing well without an edging'.

Otherwise, though, Wren largely got his way, producing a sort of Light British Baroque. He couldn't go as far as Borromini and Bernini, who filled Rome with high baroque – all swirling convex and concave curves, with dancing skylines and ever-shifting planes. That would have been far too Catholic for cool, Protestant, northern tastes.

Wren did sneak in some baroque touches – in the St Paul's dome, the rhythm of its colonnade subtly broken by stone niches (pictured, bottom right).

At Saint Vedast-alias-Foster (below left), it's thought the spire was designed by Wren's gifted young assistant, baroque master Nicholas Hawksmoor.

St Vedast's was John Betjeman's favourite spire. He loved the subtle, baroque way the lower stage is concave and the upper stage convex. He loved, too, how the light changed in the open windows of the spire as you walked by – sometimes lit by sky through the windows on the other side, sometimes in black shadow (below left).

Wren tried to realign the City's street plan with straight boulevards – as Paris and New York would later do. But the power of land law meant residents held on to their irregularly shaped, pre-Fire plots.

Thus the shiny City's steel-and-glass skyscrapers still sit on a medieval street pattern. And thus Wren's genius in fitting mighty, light-filled churches onto tiny footprints.

His masterpiece, St Stephen Walbrook, sits on the small site of the obliterated pre-Fire church.

Enter the church and you're in heaven

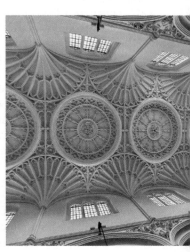

Christopher Wren's magic trick: his dome on a square, St Stephen Walbrook

are connected with pendentives (curved triangles) to produce a circle for the dome to sit on. Abracadabra!

He could really do anything. Wren could imitate pre-Fire Gothic – as at St Mary Aldermary, with its delightful, Perpendicular fan vaults; or in St Dunstan-in-the-East's flying arches, topped with a cockerel weathervane.

No two churches – or spires – were the same. Look at the steeple of St Bride's (below left), copied by an early 18th-century pastry chef, Thomas Rich, for his wedding cake – and a billion wedding cakes since. Then compare it with St Augustine Watling Street – another Hawksmoor collaboration, bombed in the Blitz, like so many Wren churches, and partially rebuilt.

The spire (pictured below) has pinnacles, each surrounded by four scary, shrieking gargoyles. Above them are four S-shaped scrolls, below elegant urns and what Angelo Hornak calls 'an elongated shallot', topped with an arrow-and-pennant weathervane. Pure joy!

Wren also employed the finest craftsmen, such as Grinling Gibbons, who died 300 years ago, in 1721.

Look at the Gibbons font cover (below left) in All Hallows by the Tower, which, like the Tower of London itself, survived the Fire. Wheat, flowers, grapes and apples are plucked by cherubs – so pudgy you want to squeeze their ultra-lifelike, limewood flesh.

For stone-carving, Wren hired Caius Gabriel Cibber, who sculpted the relief at the foot of the Monument to the Fire, showing Charles II flying in, a deus ex machina, to save the burnt-out City.

Wren built the Monument (left) to the designs of another genius, Dr Robert Hooke (as in Hooke's law of springs) – dubbed 'England's Leonardo'.

Cibber also carved the relief on St Paul's of a phoenix rising from the flames, with the Latin *RESURGAM* ('I will rise again') inscribed beneath.

Here's hoping that, as Britain and the world recover from the virus, a 21st-century Wren will rise again to lift our spirits. ◍

Angelo Hornak is author of After the Fire: London Churches in the Age of Wren, Hooke, Hawksmoor and Gibbs

– a heaven that feels surprisingly big (see above). Wren achieved this by flooding the building with light from surrounding windows and an oculus in the dome.

A Fellow of All Souls and a Professor of Astronomy at Gresham College, Wren was a brilliant mathematician. He pulls off two mathematical design tricks at St Stephen's. He places a Greek cross (with equal-length arms) at the heart of the church. And he extends it towards the entrance into a Latin cross (shaped like Christ's cross).

So you get the double effect of processing along a nave before finding yourself right at the centre of the action. It's now occupied by Henry Moore's travertine marble altar – compared by John Betjeman to a Camembert.

Wren also pulls off the trick of putting a dome on a square base by placing eight arches on eight columns. The arches

Ed McLachlan

'Well, I'm not impressed with bread and circuses so far'

Diana's first Escort

Her royal runabout has been sold for a fortune. *Roderick Gilchrist* recalls the day he bought the car and roared down the M1 in it

I had to laugh when I read that Princess Diana's old Ford Escort Ghia has just been sold at an Essex auction for £52,000.

The last time I saw the royal runabout, I was strapped into the passenger seat, terrified for my life. I was hurtling at 100mph down the M1 in the early hours of the morning in the teeth of a storm, being driven by Lord Rothermere's chauffeur, affectionately known to all as Maltese Joe.

'For God's sake, Joe,' I yelled above the crack of thunder, 'You'll smash the car and we'll both be killed. Diana wouldn't want that.'

It was April 1988 and I had just handed over £10,000 of Lord R's money for the silver Escort with the frog mascot on the bonnet to be offered to *Daily Mail* readers as a circulation-building prize. Of course the late Lord Rothermere, who owned the paper then, didn't know any of that.

Although at the time I was Executive Editor of the *Mail*, in charge of news, I had had some success suggesting competition ideas with snob appeal and strong royal association – catnip to aspiring, middle-class readers. First, at a Sotheby's auction we bought £250,000 worth of the Duchess of Windsor's jewels given to Wallis Simpson by Edward VIII before their marriage.

Next I bid £185,000 at Bonhams for the American Buick he romanced her in and indeed was driven into exile in on his last trip from Buckingham Palace.

The Windsor jewels were a runaway success, putting 100,000 new readers on the circulation every day for the five weeks. The figures were propelled by major stars of the day such as Farah Fawcett, Glynis Barber and Fiona Fullerton. They dragged up in period costume and wigs with the Cartier rocks to look like Wallis, for photo spreads in the paper.

The 1936 Buick – we dubbed it the Love Limousine of the Century – had a more bumpy ride than the jewels, breaking down three times after the sale while being driven across Blackfriars

Fit for a princess: Diana and her Ford

Bridge. Unfortunately, this was all photographed gleefully by a trailing rival snapper from the *Daily Express*, which published pictures of the stalled motor under the larky headline 'The Buick stops here … and here … and here'.

The jalopy proved to be an accident waiting to happen. While it was being filmed for a TV commercial, a giant Klieg light exploded, setting fire to the back of the car. That meant an overnight respray, before TV-am presenter Anne Diamond on her show next morning drooled live over the auto in front of the cameras. 'Whatever you do, Anne, don't touch the cellulose on air,' I warned her. 'It's still wet.'

None of these adventures prepared me for the night I was sent north to buy Diana's car. It had been a present from Charles 40 years ago, in May 1981, before the couple's 29th July wedding, and Diana continued to drive it until August 1982, after the birth of William on 21st June.

David English, then editor of the *Mail*, excited by all the drama of the jewels and the Buick, wanted me to snap up the Ford before it reached auction. He ordered me to the home of John Gibson, a gas-fitter from Leeds whose council

This was the car Diana drove in her journey from Sloane Ranger to princess

house overlooked the football ground. He had picked it up for £6,000 and wanted to turn a quick profit.

In those days, the cashiers of Associated Newspapers dolled out lolly on receipt of a signed chitty. That's how most reporters drew down their expenses, usually flaunting the greenbacks before jealous printers.

I drew £10,000 in one-pound notes because they made a bigger bundle than £20 notes – more impressive, I reckoned, when stacked together for somebody who had never seen so much money in one place. I packed all the cash into an attaché case and set off for Leeds, with Maltese Joe.

Mr Gibson, surprised by my knock at his door, welcomed me into his kitchen but initially declined my offer of spot cash, saying he preferred to go to auction.

I made it clear I wasn't prepared to haggle and flipped open the briefcase. 'Look, mate, there's ten grand there,' I told him. 'You've got 20 seconds to take it or I'm back down the motorway.'

Mr Gibson's eyes fell on the cash. He didn't even answer and just handed over the keys with a laugh.

Maltese Joe put his foot down all the way back to London, pushing the needle off the dial.

We worked the same glamour trick on the Escort as we had with the jewels and the Buick. We photographed the car Diana drove in her journey from Sloane Ranger to princess, alongside celebrities and aristos such as the actress Tracy Ward who had just married the Marquess of Worcester. The frog mascot was a bit knocked about, so we had a shiny new one fitted.

These were the golden days of Fleet Street, before the bean-counters took over and focus groups squeezed the juice out of inspired craziness.

It's sad, though, that Diana's Escort and its frog mascot, a memory-jogger from a more colourful era, is now a static museum piece – in faraway Chile, of all places. ◖

The vintage series is still gripping, says *Sara Wheeler*. It depicts a lost, dark world of capital punishment and smoking, boozing cops

Happy 60th, *Z Cars*!

The *Z Cars* crew.
Left to right:
Detective Sergeant John Watt (Frank Windsor), Detective Chief Inspector Charlie Barlow (Stratford Johns), PC Bert Lynch (James Ellis), PC Bob Steele (Jeremy Kemp)

If my childhood had a theme tune, it was *Johnny Todd*. Don't know it? Yes, you do. It was the *Z Cars* music.

The BBC detective series first beamed into our cold living rooms 60 years ago, on 2nd January 1962. Within two months, it drew in 14 million viewers. It went on to run for 801 episodes over 12 series.

Glasgow-born screenwriter Troy Kennedy Martin conceived *Z Cars* while in bed with mumps. To stave off boredom, he listened to local police messages on his transistor. Why not, he thought, bring police to life on the small screen? Why not depict bobbies as real, flawed human beings, like us?

Police presence on TV was at the time limited to the cosy *Dixon of Dock Green*, which had been running for seven years when *Z Cars* revved up. In the title role, at the start of every show, avuncular Jack Warner looked straight at the camera and greeted viewers, saying, 'Evening, all.' We thought he was talking to us.

To heighten the realism, Kennedy Martin set the series in Lancashire. TV drama seldom depicted the north. The fictional Newtown was based on Kirkby, now in Merseyside, around estates that had replaced Victorian slums and blitzed housing. Whaling ships put in at nearby Seaport, and consequences of the sailors' 'fighting beer' became a series regular. *Z Cars* folk were working class.

In the first episode, Detective Chief Inspector Charlie Barlow (Stratford Johns) and sidekick Detective Sergeant John Watt (Frank Windsor) set up a motorised unit. 'If we had crime patrols [in cars] like other divisions,' Barlow reckons, 'Reginald Farrow [a murdered colleague] would be alive today.'

In the fourth minute, this line sets out the premise of the next 800 episodes. Not everyone approved. On the front desk, tetchy Sergeant Percy Twentyman ridiculed the plan to 'take the best men off the beat and put them in those fancy cars'.

After that, storylines revolved around pairs of officers patrolling in the cars. They bet on horses, drank beer and chased women. The dapper Brian Blessed (''e ought to be in Rome') makes his first appearance as PC 'Fancy' Smith, gyrating nimbly in a dockland dance-hall doorway and leering at a girl who says she is 15. (Sadly, Bernard Holley, who played PC Newcombe, died in November, aged 81.) No wonder the Police Federation made an official complaint. The programmes were too true to life.

The series took its name from the radio call signs given to Lancashire police divisions. A Division was based in Ulverston; B Division in Lancaster. The TV series took the fictional call signs Z-Victor 1 and Z-Victor 2. The Ford Zephyr was the standard traffic-patrol car in Lancashire – the Z stood for Zulu, not Zephyr. The cars on set were primrose yellow at first, as the colour showed up better than black-and-white.

For the first three years, programmes went out live – among the last British dramas to do so. When a gloop of fried egg slithered out of PC Bert Lynch's mouth mid-sentence in the Steeles' living room as pinny-wearing Janey Steele (Dorothy White) put coal on the fire, it did so in front of 14 million viewers quietly consuming their own tea.

There could be as many as 15 sets an episode, with actors racing between

Left to right: James Ellis (Lynch), Frank Windsor (Watt), Stratford Johns (Barlow), Joseph Brady (PC Jock Weir), Colin Welland (PC Dave Graham), Robert Keegan (Sergeant Bob Blackitt), Donald Gee (PC Ray Walker)

them. Men sat in half-cars with a street projected onto a screen behind them.

I was just one when *Z Cars* began, and left home the year it ended. When I watched some episodes recently on YouTube, I was amazed, after the Proustian rush of *Johnny Todd*, at how good it remains – and how much it reveals about Britain in the early 1960s. Everyone smokes. Capital punishment is still on the statute books.

'If he's a nutcase,' Barlow says when he hears a suspect has been arrested for murdering a police colleague, 'they won't top him.'

Barlow looks the way my dad looked, though I soon realised all the men do. Besides the standard haircut, a blanched and creased postwar mien lingers.

Early on, PC Bob Steele (Jeremy Kemp) only semi-apologises for giving his wife a black eye. She responds that, at least, 'I get some respect from the neighbours now.' In other words, domestic abuse was a badge of honour and 'better', to local eyes, than a husband's 'stretch in Strangeways'.

As for the theme tune, Austrian-born Fritz Spiegl and his first wife, Bridget Fry, arranged the Liverpudlian folk ballad ('Johnny Todd, he took a notion/ For to sail the ocean wide'). When the Liverpool Music Group recorded it, with Spiegl himself conducting, it reached number two in the charts.

Another set of boys in blue, the Everton football team, adopted the anthem midway through the 1963-64

season. The Toffees won the league in 1963 and PC Ian Sweet (Terence Edmond) was an Evertonian. He suggested players run on to the tune. Thirty years later, during the 1994-95 season, club officials replaced it with *Fanfare for the Common Man*. But not for long. The Goodison faithful made their opinion clear – and back marched *Johnny Todd*.

Everyone seemed to be involved in *Z Cars*. Michael Caine turned down the role of Steele, but future Monkee Davy Jones appeared in three episodes, Leonard Rossiter in eight, and in four John Thaw played a detective constable who had to leave the force because he couldn't drink hard enough with the crims – part of the job description then.

When the original run ended in 1965, BBC executives hived off Barlow and Watt into *Softly, Softly*. After a two-year hiatus, in March 1967 *Z Cars* roared back in a twice-weekly soap format, with two 25-minute episodes forming one story.

Four years later, the BBC put both together as a single 50-minute show, and thereafter *Z Cars* alternated between two shorts and one long until settling

permanently to one 50-minute episode a week. In 1967, Pandas zoomed around the Newtown streets instead of Zephyrs, as they did in real-life Kirkby.

Kennedy Martin left the show after three episodes. Auntie felt he was going too far, and that villains had to be caught.

He was too left-wing, really – ahead of his time at the corporation. He went on to write the screenplay for *The Italian Job* in 1969 and had a hand in the fabled *Cathy Come Home*. By the late 1970s, US imports *Kojak*, *Hawaii Five-O* and *Starsky and Hutch* were ushering in a new era for police shows, and *Z Cars* parked up for the last time.

For the final episode, which went out on 20th September 1978, the BBC brought Kennedy Martin back, as well as original director John McGrath and several early cast members. The one character who remained throughout was Irishman Bert Lynch.

In a 2000 BFI poll to find the 100 greatest British TV programmes of the 20th century, the voting public put *Z Cars* at 63, between *Ready Steady Go!* and *Culloden*.

In my opinion, it should be higher. ⓦ

In the early Sixties, *Nicky Haslam*, working for *Vogue*, delivered this dazzling picture to the dazed, haunted star just before she died

My photo opportunity with Marilyn

Two indelible images were engrained in my mid-teen mind. The first was seeing, one blustery June day in 1953, the just-crowned Queen: youthfully pearlescent, sensitive, smiling through rain from that great ornate carriage as she passed, quite close, beside the windows of my father's club in St James's.

And, not very long after – having hared across those hard-won playing fields of Eton, over lanes and ditches, to the Gaumont in Slough – seeing, in celluloid colour, the world-heralded Marilyn Monroe in *There's No Business Like Show Business* (1954).

While an afternoon audience of housewives swooned at the gyrations of co-star Johnny Ray, I was enraptured by the sashaying form, the lyre-like arms, the wide luscious mouth, the *mouche* – the trembling, exquisite being that was Marilyn.

These two women, born six weeks but worlds and time and cultures apart, both young, assured and vivacious at so early a milestone in their diverse futures had, at those first *coups d'oeil*, equal promise of pleasure, security, endurance and a touching similarity in their shimmering white, diamonds and radiance.

The Queen recently confided to a friend that she'd rather longed to be an actress had statecraft not been her destiny.

But Marilyn had to contend with the pitfalls of actually being an actress in order to become queen of a more calumniatory empire.

Too soon we were to learn of the canker in Marilyn's crimson rose. Too soon came the revelations of a chaotic upbringing, deeply contorted emotions and betrayed trust. We watched, and wondered, for the next decade, at her sublime beauty, her innate goofiness, the promise of her pout, her glorious gaiety. There was always that nagging feeling that, deep down, almost nothing was right with, or for, her.

That, despite the glamour in pink satin, the black monkey fur, the swirling white and the desert-bleached denim, it was all, inevitably, a charade.

A few years pass and, while the perfection of her image remains unchanged, one's heart is in one's mouth on her behalf. She's private. She's ill. She's late. She's seeing Peter Lawford; she'll see only Natasha Lytess, her drama coach. No, she won't see anyone; she's a recluse.

The nearest I came to her was one sultry Los Angeles summer night. In a bar on Hollywood and Vine, I'd picked up a leathered hunk. Later, lazily, from his Brentwood veranda, he gestured to a one-storey across the street. 'That's Marilyn's.' He would have known: he was Peggy Lee's hairdresser.

So this was the house, pale and faded

> 'Could you take these contacts up to Miss Monroe? And wait while she chooses'

under its dusty greenery, that was to be there for the entire rocky ride, mute witness to the DiMaggio jealousy, the humiliation by Arthur Miller, the ill-fated venture with Milton Greene, the unborn child (by Tony Curtis), the clutches of the Kennedy cabal and reports of fiasco footage on the set of *Something's Gotta Give*, her unfinished last film.

A couple of Julys later, there's a conspiratorial but palpably joyous atmosphere in our art department at *Vogue* in Manhattan.

On the lay-out pinboard, among the dedicated editorial pages for the September issue, are 14 starkly white double-page spreads – no hint as to their content. The editors, Diana Vreeland, Alex Liberman and co, buzz around them proudly, congratulatorily, changing the order and shape with *sotto voce* gestures.

Whatever this project is, it's mammoth. Eventually I find out, and I am sworn to secrecy: the photographer Bert Stern has done a sensational shoot with Marilyn.

And, what's more, she's agreed to be photographed naked.

So she's all right! She's back!! On top!!! Everything's gonna be OK.

The contacts come in. Exclaimed, rhapsodised, pored over... Here she is, once again. Glorious, restored, ravishing, the honey-dewed skin, the gold-dust shoulders, the ice-white cowlick, the coral lips quivering.

Then someone remembers she has photo approval.

There's a conference, and... 'Erm,

The last picture show: Haslam handed Marilyn Monroe this Bert Stern photograph weeks before her death on 5th August 1962

Nicky' – Priscilla Peck, the art director, is the acme of politesse – 'Erm, could you, erm, take these up to Miss Monroe?' I am presented with a heavy white envelope and a red Chinagraph pencil. 'And please wait while she chooses.'

At 6.30 that evening, I ring the bell of the apartment at 444 East 57th Street. Nothing. I ring again. A small dog barks shrilly; then footsteps. The door opens. The goddess is mere inches from my eyes.

But hers are red, her greasy face and smudgy lips framed by lank, lifeless hair. She wears a shapeless grey tracksuit with make-up stains at the neckline. She looks half-dazed, almost haunted. The dog barks again. 'Be quiet, Maff,' she rasps, her hand half-shading her gaze.

I hold out the bulging envelope 'My editor has asked me to...'

'Thank you, honey, but I'm running late.' She half-closes the door, then looks down. 'Are they OK?'

'Yes, they're wonderful. Of course they're wonderful. How could they not be?'

'Oh, thank you, honey...' The mascara-messed eyes look up at me, her voice strangely remote. 'Do you mind if we look at them right here? I'm kinda...'

She opens the envelope and holds each contact sheet against the door, with the wax crayon expertly and unhesitatingly circling the ones she likes, X-ing others, and, sucking her teeth, puts a pale thumbnail through total rejects.

Just as we started on the colour transparencies, a telephone rang, faintly, in a distant room. Marilyn looked panicked. The grubby, unwashed reality gathered up these last images of her golden glory in her arms, thrust them into mine, and ran unsteadily away down the corridor. The dog barked again. The telephone stopped ringing.

Marilyn's door was still open when the elevator arrived.

She died three weeks later. ◐

Jilly Cooper's advice on keeping up with female pals?
Treat them like tennis balls. By *Claire Cohen*

A guide to lady friends

Jilly Cooper recently gave me a precious insight into her writing process.

'Trust in the unexpected,' she said cheerily. I scribbled it on a Post-it note and stuck it to my computer screen, hoping it might temporarily grant me even one per cent of her literary prowess as I embarked on my own first book. Jilly's message could apply to almost every aspect of my subject: female friendship.

From our earliest days in the playground, our connections with other girls consume our waking thoughts. We spend our days trying to make friends and devote time to second-guessing their every move. Whether they think we're best friends or prefer Sally in Form 5. If we'll be invited to their birthday party.

Before romantic relationships, childhood friendships are the most emotionally fraught and rewarding connections outside our families – and they can continue that way throughout our lives, particularly for women.

Dr Anna Machin, an evolutionary anthropologist at the University of

Friends reunited: *Thelma & Louise* (1991)

Oxford who has studied female friendship, says that, for an increasing number of women, friendships are our 'survival-critical relationships'. In other words, whether we marry and have families or not, it's our female friends who will offer the security, support and influence over the big decisions that are central to our lives.

More than that, Dr Machin reported her 'surprise' at her unexpected discovery: women get more emotionally intimate, can more easily be themselves and have more in common with their female friends than with male romantic partners.

The same doesn't – in general – tend to be true of friendships between men. They often don't seek friendships in the way women do, she explained. As another Oxford professor put it of men, 'So long as the other person is capable of holding a pint glass to their lips, that's good enough.'

Female friendships often change shape as life progresses. It's something few of us are prepared for – having been, I believe, sold a myth in our younger years that best friends are for ever.

The truth is messier. As life's milestones creep up on us – job changes, moves, falling in love, children, illness, divorce and death – friendship gaps open up, as our circumstances are no longer aligned. We can drift. The expectations we have of one another (that your friends might be busy much of the time, but will be there when the proverbial hits the fan)

can be tested and come up short.

I interviewed women whose childhood friends hadn't been there for them when a parent died, or when their husband walked out; or who had cut them off after a few cross words.

Maintaining a platonic bond with another person for a decade, two, three … it's a serious achievement we don't really take the time to acknowledge.

We should. While the other loving relationships in our lives tend to be bound by blood ties or legal documents, our friendships are entirely conditional. Every time you pick up the phone, write a card or make a date, you're making an active choice to keep that person in your life through little else but loyalty, respect, enjoyment and mutual support.

And with friends you've had since childhood, university, your first flatshare or first job? It's all the more remarkable how they can endure. 'You just pick them up again like a tennis ball and have lovely fun with them,' as Jilly told me.

Provided, that is, those old friends uphold their end of the bargain. Many of us have had a long-term friendship turn sour because one party struggles not to keep the other in a box.

The good news is it's never too late to make new friends, rekindle friendships following those 'gaps' or even make 'old friends'.

Helge Rubinstein, 91, told me about her 70-year friendship with Shirley Williams. She said she had made 'old friends' later in life with people who were acquaintances years before. They suddenly took on a more important role as her close friends sadly died.

Helge said, 'I'm making not new friends, but old friends. People I knew and might have had dinners with, but didn't know well, have become friends. And that's a weird, but rather nice process.'

And I'm not sure there's a stronger endorsement for the unexpected nature of female friendship than that. ◍

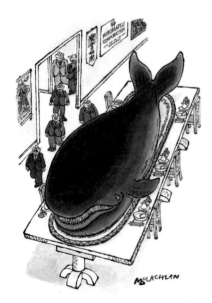

'It'll be typical Japanese meal I expect – we'll be hungry an hour later.'

History

Happy 200th birthday, Flashy!

The Flashman books are a masterclass in historical fiction

DAVID HORSPOOL

The 200th anniversary of the birth of Sir Harry Flashman VC has been greeted with an outpouring of affection and admiration. You can imagine the old rogue laughing off the adulation, while inwardly relishing it all.

And yes, I know, unlike those allegedly credulous American first reviewers, that Flashman wasn't real. For all his creator George MacDonald Fraser's meticulous research and poker-faced footnotes to the Flashman Papers, the novels follow the fortunes of a fictional character of someone else's invention – Thomas Hughes.

Hughes had already muddied the waters by including a real figure in *Tom Brown's Schooldays*, the headmaster Dr Thomas Arnold, who expels Flashman from Rugby for drunkenness.

It's a nice question whether the roguery or the research made Flashman such a triumph. My money is, just, on the research, if only because a baddie protagonist is not essential to a successful historical novel. The best historical fiction is always anchored in reality, and most historical novelists agree that the trick is not to change the facts, but to imagine a new route between them.

Operating in the shadowy territory between the known and unknown is standard practice. But what often marks out the really successful historical novelist is something historians do their best to avoid: anachronism.

I don't mean having Mary Queen of Scots book in for a blow-dry, but the more or less subtle introduction of sensibilities from our time into the past. Often, too, these instances are a reaction to the work of straight historians.

Take Flashman. One of the reasons we can find the Victorians difficult to stomach is that they were so damned earnest. Bent on improving everything from sewage to schools, they were so steeped in self-belief that they were convinced of their right, or even duty, to export their methods to every part of the globe. Flashman lets us see more plainly than any Lytton Strachey that the whole thing is, if not a façade, then a mostly malign muddle.

Here he is in *Flashman and the Mountain of Light* (a book named for the diamond the British 'acquired' at the same time as the Punjab):

'You'll have heard it said that the British Empire was acquired in a fit of absence of mind – one of those smart, Oscarish squibs that sounds well but is thoroughly fat-headed. Presence of mind, if you like – and countless other things, such as greed and Christianity, decency and villainy, policy and lunacy, deep design and blind chance, blunder and curiosity, passion, ignorance, chivalry and expediency, honest pursuit of right, and determination to keep the bloody Frogs out.'

The reference to 'absence of mind' is to the 19th-century imperial historian J R Seeley. While Seeley was in part making a case that the British should think a lot harder about their imperial duties, the idea that they had come by them accidentally appealed to a people who didn't like to think of themselves as too domineering. Flashy lets us know it's all rot.

The fact that we hardly notice the novelist speaking through his creation here – and giving us a history lesson – is further testimony to Fraser's genius.

Robert Graves had done something similar for his view of the Roman Empire in *I, Claudius* and its sequel. One of Graves's motivations (along with all the money he made from the books) was the belief 'that the story has been mistold by history'. He didn't choose a villain to

King of the rogues

retell it but, like Fraser, he chose to recast his history through a memoir.

Claudius was an emperor whom Suetonius, Tacitus and Cassius Dio had portrayed as an idiot or a weakling. Graves also foreshadows Fraser's insistence on the 'genuineness' of his discovery, including tricky translation questions in a note (for which he consulted 'Aircraftman T E Shaw', better known as Lawrence of Arabia, and a keen classicist who translated the *Odyssey*).

The rehabilitation of Claudius involved dragging his predecessor Caligula's name even deeper into the mire. The process was completed by a TV adaptation that had John Hurt's Caligula ripping a baby from the womb and eating it – an atrocity neither Graves nor his ancient sources had invented.

The idea of historical reputation as a zero-sum game – if there is a winner, there must be a loser – has been on show most recently in Hilary Mantel's *Wolf Hall* novels.

Mantel's Thomas Cromwell is another figure history has 'got wrong'. In her rebalancing, it is Thomas More who finds himself at the other end of the seesaw.

Again, creative anachronism is at work. Mantel's Cromwell – loyal, empathetic and only occasionally ruthless – is not much like the character contemporaries or historians have given us. But he suits our age perfectly – much better than the saintly fanatic Thomas More.

Like Flashman and Claudius, Mantel's Cromwell makes us question our historical assumptions. They all remind us that, however much we think we know about a historical figure, we never know what they were thinking. ◑

After seeing a show of Ardizzone's drinking pictures, *Hugh Thompson* staggers around London pubs in his footsteps

My 1939 pub crawl

In 1939, the illustrator Edward Ardizzone (1900-79) combined with his friend Maurice Gorham, a journalist (1902-75), to produce *The Local*. In 1947, there was a sequel, *Back to the Local*.

Beginning at their base in Maida Vale, it was a guide to pubs, their customs and culture.

There are chapters on the regulars, barmaids, saloon and public bars, outside and inside eating, drunks, musicians and after-hours drinking.

A recent show at the Christ Beetles Gallery in London included a marvellous picture of a barmaid by Ardizzone. The artist Paul Cox has, like me, done a pilgrimage around the same pubs and painted them – those pictures were also in the show.

I was at the same school as Ardizzone, Clayesmore in Dorset. He was there from 1914 to 1919. My old schoolfriend Stephen Dover and I (both class of 1964) thought it might be fun to check up on the differences between then and now.

First, the Prince Alfred near Warwick Avenue tube (*pictured, by Paul Cox*). Ardizzone would have been delighted that the architecture, windows and bars and the way they have been divided are very much as he would have seen them.

Today, there are no public or saloon bars, though the 'cavernous architectural saloons' are still very much there, complete with frosted windows, carved partitions and 'crouch-down' connecting doorways.

Games have long since gone, with darts and cribbage a distant memory. Board games were played before COVID but haven't come back. The area once reserved for darts-playing is no more.

And the men in flat caps have gone the same way. Funnily enough, in 1939, *The Local* despaired of the craze for darts changing the character of pubs,

Top: Barmaid in the Alma by Ardizzone. **Bottom: The Prince Alfred** by Paul Cox

Ardizzone's pub drawings. *Above left: The Goat. Above: Darts at the Alfred. Left: The Warrington Lounge*

'but the worst dangers seemed to have passed away'.

The barmaids of Ardizzone's day have been replaced by a charming Greek chap, Ilias, who has been there two years.

He reported that the pub's business is mainly locals and mostly at weekends, especially at Sunday lunchtime, when the place is heaving.

On the Wednesday lunchtime we visited, there were only a dozen people in a pub designed for ten times that number. We gave the food, in terms of quality and value, 7/10. And a higher mark for the ale.

Next we went to the Spread Eagle, just off Oxford Street. Eighty years ago, the pub was famous for its barmaids: they were 'there to attract men and anxious to please … at the Spread Eagle, two dizzy blondes both sprang forward as soon as you opened the door'.

In the book, as a West End pub, it was likely to suffer from Bright Young People, the Flash Trade chasing out the Regulars and then deserting and leaving behind a wreck – 'an awful warning for the licensed trade'.

The Spread Eagle's dining room was then representative of 'smaller restaurants that are truly part of the pub but they are discreetly segregated from the bars'.

Architecturally, little has changed at the Spread Eagle. For 22 years, this Greene King pub has been run by the totally charming Liverpudlians Paul and Elaine. There was banter about when the dizzy blondes would appear. They didn't.

Typically, the pub gets its regulars from the tourists and shoppers who flow up and down Oxford Street. Neither were very apparent. But that Friday lunchtime the pub had a good crowd.

What would have depressed old-school Ardizzone was that this is now a football pub. Paul, a Liverpool fan, has installed the TV screens that gave the pub another strand of business.

Just as in 1939, a limited menu was well served. The steak pies had rich gravy, as they would have before the war.

Then it was off to the Goat (*pictured, by Ardizzone*) off Old Bond Street. In *The Local*, it is famous for 'its modest exterior and cosy private bar'.

Gorham was pleased the pub avoided the dread 'young men about town with curled moustaches and a lot of shirt-cuff, and dress designers and photographers' models', the kind of people who were (for Ardizzone) ruining West End pubs. In the saloon bar, there were reproductions of horse prints and caricatures of the landlord. The landlord 'chats to the habitués. Dalliance with the barmaids is practised.'

The pub is still a very traditional mini-pub. It's now run by a Polish lady called Daga and Anthony from Deptford. Anthony was only two weeks into the job, while Daga had been there some time. She loved that every day was different. She knew her regulars' names; they were like family. After five years with Greene King, she is now an assistant manageress.

The last stop was the Warrington Hotel (*pictured, by Ardizzone*), Maida Vale. This was the grandest of the four stops in our mini pub crawl.

In 1939, *The Local* called it 'a landmark – a fine building that dominates a whole neighbourhood. It has not rested on its laurels.' It had, as now, just been 'furbished'. An illuminated sign then proclaimed it as 'London's liveliest lounge bar'.

In the illustration of the Warrington in *The Local*, men and women are lolling or going upstairs, suggesting there were assignations going on. The present owners admit that at one time it had a reputation for that sort of thing.

So, on a Tuesday lunchtime, the two Old Clayesmorians approached. While the bar was not exactly bursting, there was much to enjoy: Victorian architecture to die for, murals rarely seen, priceless mosaics, stained glass of international standard, marble arches and tiled fireplaces… Ardizzone would have felt at home.

Other pubs had shown the dizzy barmaid was a feature of the past. But at the Warrington, there was Jane: big, buxom, friendly, tattooed and fun.

Now assistant manageress, she has worked in pubs all her life and has two children in their early twenties who are following in her footsteps. She said business was getting back to normal. Popular bands played to full houses on Saturday nights. And the hotel's five bedrooms were nearly always full.

She made our day. ◑

Back to the Local by Maurice Gorham, illustrated by Edward Ardizzone, is published by Faber

Gyles Brandreth's Diary

The King and I

What a Coronation! There were lots of loos, Emma Thompson saved a choirboy – and I stole Lionel Richie's seat

Our new king is a Shakespeare buff, so quite familiar with the famous line spoken by Francisco on the ramparts at Elsinore at the beginning of *Hamlet*: 'For this relief, much thanks.'

This line was repeated by quite a few of us oldies lucky enough to be invited to the Coronation as we arrived at Westminster Abbey and found the ancient building almost surrounded by Portaloos.

There had been a rumour that 'facilities' would be in short supply at the royal peculiar. People were upping the pre-crowning bladder panic by repeating apocryphal tales of 'accidents' that had occurred at the last Coronation in 1953. The *Daily Mail* called me to ask if I would contribute a feature they were hoping to headline 'The Royal Wee'.

I declined, and how wise I was. Every aspect of the Coronation was brilliantly organised. The Dean and his ever good-humoured and consistently courteous team had thought of everything. There were ramps for the wheelchairs, smelling salts for the faint, defibrillators in the side chapels and clean and classy, unobtrusively placed toilets at every turn.

When things went awry on the day, it certainly wasn't the fault of the organisers. We were invited to take our places from 7.30am and advised that we shouldn't expect to leave until 1.30pm. I cut it a bit fine arriving at 8.30am and took what I thought was my place – only to be told, moments later, by the great Lionel Richie that, actually, it was his.

In the event, amazingly, I found

Right royal day: Emma Thompson; Norroy and Ulster King of Arms; Gyles

myself at the end of a row of hugely distinguished old soldiers – all recipients of either the George Cross or the VC – and just behind the actress Dame Emma Thompson, who deserves an extra gong for services rendered on the day.

As the 14-year-old Child of His Majesty's Chapel Royal, Samuel Strachan, began to address the King, someone halfway along Dame Emma's row began coughing. And went on coughing. Loudly. And more loudly still.

Emma reached for her handbag, found her packet of Bronchostops and passed them down the line.

Happily, I don't think there were any medical emergencies on the day. Had there been, there were plenty in the congregation ready to come to the rescue.

After the service, walking towards Victoria Station, I fell into step with one of them. She was a retired nurse, she told me – and then, seeing her medals, I realised she was Dame Elizabeth Anionwu, the UK's first sickle-cell specialist nurse and the first nurse to receive the Order of Merit since Florence Nightingale. An hour before, she had been carrying the Orb of Sovereignty in the Coronation procession. Now she was walking on her own along the Embankment in the rain with me. I felt proud to be British.

I felt proud, too, of my buttonhole.

To my surprise, it was the only one I noticed in the Abbey.

It was made up of four miniature, cream-coloured roses I had pinched from a beautiful arrangement of flowers the day before and kept fresh in the fridge overnight.   My Coronation buttonhole came from *Coronation Street*. Truly, it did. I am a regular on ITV's *This Morning* and, naturally, our Coronation Special came from Salford, from the set of the longest-running soap in the kingdom.

At the end of the broadcast, as William Roache (aka Ken Barlow), 91, who has been in the series since it started in 1960, led us in three cheers for King Charles.

I discreetly dismembered the floral arrangement that was decorating the bar of the Rovers Return.

I have been partial to a buttonhole since I was a boy.

One day in the mid-1950s, as I was walking along the Strand with my father, we caught sight of an elegant gentleman getting out of a London taxi and stepping in to the Savoy Hotel.

'That,' said my dad, 'is the great Nubar Gulbenkian – he wears a fresh orchid in his buttonhole every day.'

He also wore a monocle, a long bushy beard and (can I have invented this?) spats.

Born in the Ottoman Empire in 1896, he was educated at Harrow and Cambridge, inherited a fortune and made another one, did good stuff for British intelligence during the Second World War, and behaved as he felt an English gentleman should.

My dad called Gulbenkian 'the Armenian Noël Coward' and collected his quips. Gulbenkian owned two converted taxis and said of them proudly, 'They can turn on a sixpence – whatever that is.'

He enjoyed fine dining, claiming 'The best number for a dinner party is two – myself and a damn good head waiter.' He was married three times: 'I've had good wives, as wives go, and, as wives go, two of them went.'

On Coronation Day, I channelled my inner Nubar. ◑

RESTAURANTS
JAMES PEMBROKE
LAST LUNCH WITH MY FATHER

My father died on New Year's Eve, aged 87.

He deserves all the credit for my lifelong obsession with restaurants, because we ate out pretty much every night during my childhood. The only time I was told I was spoilt was when, aged four, I demanded ice cream, and wailed at the waitress, 'And don't you dare bring me a wafer.' I have hated them ever since.

It never occurred to my parents or me that we were spoilt, eating our way through the seventies at Hungry Horse, Borsch N Tears, Le Bistingo, Halepi or Bertorelli.

Every night was theatre, especially if we went to Flanagans and sang along with the pianist. By the age of six, I was precociously menu-literate, flipping between boeuf bourguignon and duck à l'orange. Even during our weekends in our heavenly, slug-smeared cottage in Dorset, we ate out for lunch and dinner while the more perfect dads loaded barons of beef into their Volvos.

I now know that all this dining out was run through my father's City business. Just about everything was: even holidays abroad were for research. My first school fees went through the books because the bill came not from Spyway School but from the headmaster brothers, E and G Warner.

My father's bookkeeper assumed they were a firm of stationers, and for four painless years my father never corrected him. I remember his woe when, after the school closed, the next bill arrived more accurately from the Old Malthouse School. Still, this urban Pa Larkin could always restore his equilibrium with lunch at the Contented Sole or Sweetings.

He was a surprisingly slim man and rejoiced in the role of the Charles Atlas of Swanage beach, where his own gastronomic career began during the war at his Aunt Nancy's hotel, the Wolfeton. No slouch in the kitchen, she got the hotel into one of 91 slots in the first-ever *Good Food Guide* in 1951.

He had no interest in making friends, and was bemused by the concept of seeing anyone regularly, but my father revelled in the sociability of restaurants and pubs.

He was only too happy to talk to neighbouring tables in London or on holiday, heckling them with his views on his pet topics, Charles and Di in the nineties and Madeleine McCann in the noughties. While his various audiences regaled him with their own conspiracy theories, he would suddenly burst out laughing at his own sense of the absurd before delivering another well-honed soliloquy on Edwina Currie and John Major.

My last lunch with him was in September at the Pier Head, overlooking Swanage Bay. Like a boy released from boarding school, he leapt out of the car, forgetting he was tethered to a small oxygen tank the size of a fire extinguisher.

It was the weekend of the Folk Festival; a passing troupe of Morris dancers untangled him and sat him down. We had a massive sea bass for just £38, he still adhering to his childhood rule of eating all the vegetables first.

Like me, he wasn't a perfect dad, but he didn't mind a bit. When my brother and I were small, he loved to ask us, 'Would you prefer this daddy or another daddy?' And he delighted in our guaranteed response: 'ANOTHER DADDY.'

I've changed my mind. ◑

Genius 295 - solution
From page 68

For 40 years, Barry Humphries wrote to *Roger Lewis* about
John Betjeman, Oscar Wilde – and the Grim Reaper

Barry's last words

I'm getting to be like John Gielgud, when he lamented, 'All my real friends are dead' – Michael Winner, Bryan Forbes, Barry Cryer and now Barry Humphries.

I knew Barry for about 40 years, ever since I interviewed him for a colour supplement. We subsequently met in odd spots of his own choosing, such as the Freud Museum in Hampstead, where he reclined on the couch – or the National Galley in Wales, so he could point at a picture by Anton Mauve and remark on the coincidental use of mauve paint.

Served a meagre portion of pie in the cafeteria of a veteran car museum in Coventry, he said to the waitress, 'Has news of my diet reached the kitchen?'

I miss him terribly – he was a sort of father figure, whose approval and admiration I always sought.

'I enjoy all you put your pen to, whereas my maladroit sentences seem to announce my decline,' he said to me once.

Far from it – his letters and (latterly) emails I will always prize, and was proud to receive. He also wrote, 'We're off to Australia on Wednesday and, like all old men going upstairs or opening the fridge, I can't remember why.'

Usually, our correspondence revolved around artists and authors. 'I used to haunt the Gotham Book Mart in the hope of getting a glimpse of Edward Gorey and instead I met Salvador Dalí.' Or 'I went to Hove with John Betjeman to meet Bosie, who talked of the races. We couldn't divert this stream of turf talk.'

Wilde often turned up in out chat. Barry didn't appreciate Rupert Everett's biopic. 'It was all about the agony and ecstasy of pillow-biting. A few of Oscar's quips chucked in and a few totally apocryphal scenes, like in the pub where he sings *The Boy I Love Is Up in the Gallery* to a spellbound audience of Frogs in fancy dress. It's shithouse.'

NEIL SPENCE

Barry Humphries (17th February 1934-22nd April 2023) at his Hampstead home in 2021

A card for Roger, Dieppe Opera House, 1977

He was good at being caustic, like this on Victoria Wood: 'The worst work I've ever done was when I was trying to be liked. I'm not good at it, but I've fooled a lot of people. Victoria was exceptionally likeable. That epithet would be a posthumous insult if it ever cropped up in my obituaries. So would be "delightful".'

He was highly attentive to language: 'Have you noticed the current modish word is "unprecedented"?'

Another expression he hated was "to be honest", "perfectly honest" or "absolutely honest", which Barry thought portended dishonesty, mendacity. 'Oh and what about all those inclusive TV commercials? They are so conspicuously inclusive, you wonder why they don't include Eskimos or Kalahari bushmen. Racism, I presume.'

Political correctness, of course, set him off. He'd not be told by anyone.

When he was notoriously cancelled by the Melbourne Comedy Festival a few years ago, he told me, 'The Barry was always a silly name for a comedy award. Perhaps the Lezzo has a more accurate ring.'

He signed petitions in support of J K Rowling, who was in the soup with the transgender mob. 'It is pitiful we have to go out on a very dangerous limb to defend the truth. By condemning the Stasi who excoriate JKR, we are now on the blacklist.'

Yet Barry never stopped working. There was, for example, what he called a 'non-event' with Rob Brydon at the Palladium, where he had to discuss his favourite cinematic comedy moments, introducing clips. 'I can't think of any, except the cabin scene in *A Night at the Opera* or the dwarf in *Don't Look Now*. I thought the pram and governess scene in *Battleship Potemkin* might be risible and the green-chunder scene in *The Exorcist*.'

I recommended Shelley Winters swimming underwater in *The Poseidon Adventure*. 'Thanks to you, the subaqueous Shelley made an appearance,' he reported the next day. 'That Sheila can certainly hold her breath.'

During lockdown, Barry dodged the curfews and went to Cornwall, 'to Zennor, where I fell off the cliff in March 1962. The helicopter rescue made the national news.' All the rules and restrictions made him nervous. 'Skulking

'The worst work I've ever done was when I was trying to be liked'

about does make one feel a bit Jewish, like dodging the patrols in Vichy France.'

He never liked the sound of Hastings, where I've lived since 2018. 'What's at the end of your pier? A derelict theatre? A palm-reader? Michael Kitchen and Honeysuckle Weeks? It's not for you. You might bump into Inspector Foyle, but otherwise it's a depressing place, like all those other sinks on the South Coast, full of cheap B&Bs and whiffy retirement homes, reeking of old roasts, cabbage and rarely changed Depends … You'd be better off in Sidmouth.'

He then added, 'Sydney Harbour looks very grey this morning – so I think I'll give Larkin's letters a miss.'

Then, in January, the bad news came. 'God has touched the pause button on my life. Various ills and inconveniences have assailed me since before Christmas. I ended up in Sydney being devoured by an enormous Siemens scanner. The company that funded Hitler's election had discovered tumours in my spine.

'This desolate news is just for you. I felt somehow I should tell you. They have zapped me, and the doctors are hopeful. I'm surrounded by little nurses from Galway and Manila. The doc says I can't go back to London until late March, but who'd be in a hurry to go back there anyway?'

In April, he said, 'Just entered my fourth month in hospital. They say I'm nearly out, but I've heard that before. I loll here like an odalisque watching old TV shows – London as it was a couple of years after I got there. Not much traffic, pretty and forgotten dolly birds, sideburns, flared pants and impossible baddies. Wonderful action stuff really performed by the actors.'

It got worse. I had a heart attack; he broke his hip. 'I'm horrified to hear your desolate news. Now is not Our Time. What a pity we're not in the same institution. The supernatural is all we have to rely on and it never lets us down and even if it does, we are completely unaware of it.

'With love to you and dear Anna. Your bedridden friend, Barry.' ◐

Larry Grayson, born 100 years ago, was a child actor, female impersonator – and national treasure. By *Christopher Sandford*

Shut that door!

In the swim: on *The Larry Grayson Show*, 1977

Y ou might think a birth name of William White, which as a boy he shortened to Willie White, had quite enough comic potential for an entertainer who later brought high camp to British television.

But, in the end, he rejected it for the *nom de panto* Larry Grayson.

William was born, out of wedlock, on 31st August 1923. He never knew his father and grew up with a foster family in Nuneaton, Warwickshire, where his mother sometimes visited him as 'Aunt' Ethel.

Then his foster mother died when he was just six years old, leaving him in the care of her two adolescent daughters.

His childhood may have had its Dickensian side, but it also supplied many of the real-life models for his later comic monologues featuring the likes of Apricot Lil, Pop-it-in-Pete the postman, and Slack Alice, the coalman's daughter with her Black Bottom.

Leaving school at 14, William made his stage debut at a local working men's club, singing a number called *In the Bushes at the Bottom of the Garden*. Both it, and his later repertoire, were a veritable dictionary of musical innuendo.

From there, using the name Billy Breen, he went on to develop a variety act as a female impersonator, sashaying around in a knee-length frock and a beret. Delivering his lines with pursed

lips and fluttering eyes, he was as high camp as a row of Alpine tents.

A few years later, he changed his stage name for the final time, taking the surname of the *Show Boat* star Kathryn Grayson, and adding 'Larry' because he liked the sound of it.

Grayson spent the next 30 years slogging his way through clubland, honing his brand of slightly surreal, observational comedy.

Some of his trademark catchphrases took root as a direct result of his working environment. 'Look at the muck on 'er' originated when he followed a parrot impersonator – or a real parrot, in some accounts – out on stage.

'Shut that door!' – his most famous

ITV / SHUTTERSTOCK

On *The Larry Grayson Show* and, *left*, with the Lochiel Marching Band of Scotland on *The Generation Game* in 1978

catchphrase – came when he felt a sudden draught while performing at a seaside theatre in Redcar. Grayson instinctively shouted the phrase, got a laugh and kept using it.

A gentle and genuinely shy man, Grayson was in some ways an unlikely candidate to be a public entertainer, let alone one who pranced around the nation's provincial clubs and holiday camps in a frock before finally hitting the big time in his fifties.

Post-war British audiences may have enjoyed a good drag act, but the times as a whole were still inhospitable to openly gay performers. Perhaps, as a result, Grayson preferred to keep his personal life quiet.

The closest he ever came to a love match was with a Nuneaton school friend called Tom Proctor, who was killed in action at the Battle of Monte Cassino in 1944, at the age of 21. Grayson never got over the loss.

His only live-in companion in later life was his beloved foster sister and surrogate mother, Florence, known as Fan, although he was once rather improbably said to have been engaged to the actress Noele Gordon of *Crossroads* fame.

'Larry and sex just didn't go together,' says his former manager, Paul Vaughan. 'I remember when gay activists were trying to out him, and two of them came in to meet him in his dressing room. He just sat there with his poodle, Arthur Marshall, and said, "Now what's all this about?"

'One of them said, "Mr. Grayson, we just want you to come out and say you're a homosexual." Immediately Larry put his hands over Arthur's ears and said, "Ooh, you can't use language like that in front of my dog."'

Grayson's big break came in 1972, when the ATV boss Lew Grade signed him up for his Saturday night variety show, before giving him his own 16-part series, *Shut That Door!* Actually, it was more like a door opening.

When Bruce Forsyth left the BBC in 1978, Grayson took over as host of *The Generation Game*, which was soon trouncing Forsyth's rival ITV show *The Big Night* in the ratings.

An engaging mixture of observational humour, sexually ambiguous jokes and good, old-fashioned show business oomph, it once attracted an audience of 25 million viewers, although admittedly the competing channel was out on strike at the time.

Unusually, it was Grayson himself, not the network executives, who ended his tenure on *The Generation Game* in 1982, citing his desire to 'go out on top' – another line he delivered with a knowing roll of his eyes.

After a series of only fitfully successful comebacks, Grayson made his final television appearance on 3rd December 1994, as part of the *Royal Variety Performance* recently filmed at the Dominion Theatre in London.

'You thought I was dead!' he commented from the stage, referring to his long absence from the nation's screens. Sadly, only a month after the show's transmission, he actually was dead, after suffering a fatal haemorrhage at his Nuneaton home in the early hours of 7th January 1995. He was 71.

Grayson never quite became an international superstar, although he had his moments, and was obviously reluctant to be a spokesman for anyone's causes.

'Endearing' was the usual verdict, upgraded in the polite obituaries to 'beloved national treasure'. ◐

Christopher Sandford is author of The Man Who Would Be Sherlock: The Real Life Adventures of Arthur Conan Doyle

Arts & Crafts

UK Travel

Genealogy

Overseas Travel

Gifts

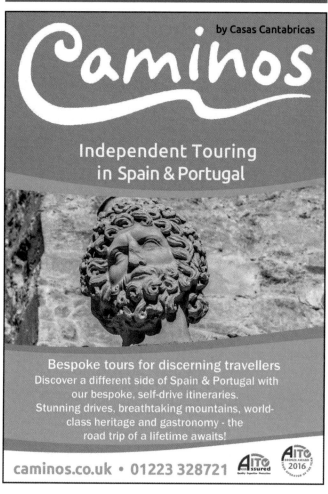

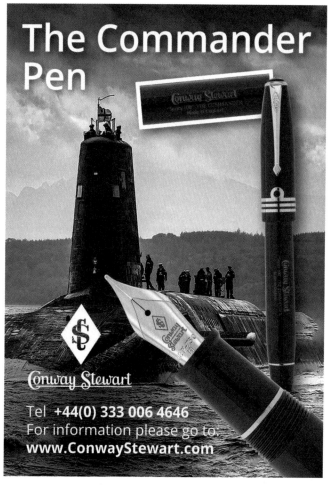

Genealogy

The ◎ldie Emporium

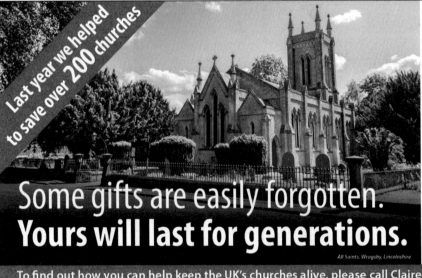